Love & Grief

Find Healing, Meaning, and Purpose in Life after Loss

Emily P. Bingham

wellfleet
press

© 2024 by Quarto Publishing Group USA Inc.
Text © 2024 by Emily P. Bingham

First published in 2024 by Wellfleet Press,
an imprint of The Quarto Group,
142 West 36th Street, 4th Floor,
New York, NY 10018, USA
T (212) 779-4972 F (212) 779-6058
www.Quarto.com

Wellfleet Press titles are also available at discount for retail, wholesale, promotional, and bulk purchase. For details, contact the Special Sales Manager by email at specialsales@quarto.com or by mail at
The Quarto Group, Attn: Special Sales Manager,
100 Cummings Center Suite 265D, Beverly, MA 01915 USA.

10 9 8 7 6 5 4 3 2 1

ISBN: 978-1-57715-400-6

Digital edition published in 2024
eISBN: 978-0-7603-8575-3

Library of Congress Control Number: 2023942841

Publisher: Rage Kindelsperger
Creative Director: Laura Drew
Editorial Director: Erin Canning
Managing Editor: Cara Donaldson
Editor: Amy Lyons
Cover Design: Clare Skeats
Book Layout: Danielle Smith-Boldt

Printed in China

This book provides general information on various widely known and widely accepted images that tend to evoke feelings of strength and confidence. However, it should not be relied upon as recommending or promoting any specific diagnosis or method of treatment for a particular condition, and it is not intended as a substitute for medical advice or for direct diagnosis and treatment of a medical condition by a qualified physician. Readers who have questions about a particular condition, possible treatments for that condition, or possible reactions from the condition or its treatment should consult a physician or other qualified healthcare professional.

For Ian, Izzy, and Theo.

Contents

My Story

As a teen, I remember wondering why terrible things never happened to me. At my ripe old age of sixteen, I witnessed accounts of peers struggling with eating disorders, sexual abuse, parents dying, or some other trauma that, to me, felt like a distant dream.

I questioned *why?* Why was I the one spared from enduring these hardships? It didn't seem fair that I didn't have to suffer; that life treated me well.

Even though I could have easily been the victim of similar tragedies, I never imagined that they could happen to me. I felt immune to hardship, struggle, and darkness . . . until March 26, 2019, when my thirty-two-year-old husband, Ian, passed away from cancer, leaving me as a solo mom of two and living a life of struggle, hardship, and darkness that felt *less* like that distant dream, and *more* like my worst nightmare.

How did I thrive—not just survive—in the aftermath of his death? That's what this book is about, and we will dive into it all shortly!

A key concept that has truly shifted the story of my husband's death from one of tragedy to resilience, transformation, and inspiration is meaning-making. Using my experience of loss to help others has given my husband's death new meaning. And in the phases of acute grief, as I wondered how the heck I was going to put my life back together, I leaned on the words of other widows and stories of other people's suffering to help me endure my own.

Inspired by this concept, I started to share my story. Within months, I began connecting with widows, bereaved mothers—total strangers—on the internet about my experience of loss and how I was navigating grief. As they told me how my story helped them heal, I was able to heal myself.

This exchange of mutual healing motivated me to launch my business moveTHRU nine months after my husband's death. At the time I was a spin instructor, and instead of talk therapy, sweat therapy had become my primary tool for coping with the big emotions in grief. When I felt paralyzed by the reality of my new normal, I could take back power by moving my body!

Through exercise I could embody my emotions—feel them and release them—in a way that I couldn't through talk therapy. So I started teaching grief movement classes in my local spin studio, launched an online course, and hosted my first ever online grief group.

I wasn't just moving through my own grief anymore—I had started a full-blown movement supporting and empowering others to move through theirs by connecting them with a community who could understand what they were going through. With hundreds of thousands of followers on social media, clients enrolling in my programs, and a methodology co-created with a licensed clinical therapist, I decided to invest further in grief coaching.

I wanted to learn tools, models, and modalities to help clients re-build their lives after a loss. I trained with the Institute for Life Coaching and got my Grief Educator Certification from Grief Expert David Kessler, and I continue to invest in my training and education to this day.

The insights, tools, and practices outlined in the book are largely influenced by David Kessler's commitment to grief education and his lifelong work in the space, as well as positive psychology, somatic practices, and creative insights inspired by my own journey through grief.

My grief has changed in the years since Ian's passing. Heavy sadness and longing now feel like deep gratitude and acceptance. As you will discover in the pages of this book, grief never goes away . . . it shapeshifts and evolves. In fact, I love my grief now! By learning to flow with it, feel it, and embrace it, I've been able to integrate my loss, and in doing so, a whole new way of living has opened up for me.

In this world, duality exists! Light is amplified by the darkness. Beginnings start with some sort of end. Rebirth by nature requires death. This binary relationship is reflected through the human experience.

I'm at peace with the fact that terrible things happen . . . not to just others, but to me too. And moving forward, I know I am not immune to more tragedy wreaking havoc in my life.

I haven't always seen the world as this unpredictable, chaotic, and random place. But the experience of navigating my husband's life-treating cancer diagnosis, surrendering to his ultimate death, and figuring out how to put back all the pieces of my life not just to survive in the aftermath of loss, but to thrive . . . I've had to shift my entire perspective around the world. Who I am in it? And what I want to accomplish here, viscerally knowing that my time is finite?

And do you know what?

I'm BETTER for it!

Yes, I said it. My experience of suffering has made me a better human. And no, it does not minimize the tragedy or act as any consolation for losing my husband, my soulmate, my children's father, and my best friend, Ian. It's just that BOTH truths can exist!

You can suffer tremendous loss AND become more grateful. You can endure profound pain AND become more resilient. You can walk through darkness AND become a beacon of light. I know, because I have! My clients have! My hundreds of thousands of followers on social media have as well. And the reason I wrote this book is so you can too.

THE 6 Cs OF GRIEF

The 6 Cs are key concepts that will bring you support and empowerment as you move through grief. I've implemented them in my own grief journey and helped clients apply them to theirs. I'll sprinkle them throughout the book, but here's a breakdown before we get started!

1. Curiosity

You may feel the tendency to be down on yourself during grief. There are a lot of new feelings and experiences that make you feel like you're doing everything wrong, but instead of criticizing yourself, I invite you to get curious! Get curious about your emotions—what are they telling you? Get curious about grief and other people's experiences. Learn as much as you can. There's so much additional, unnecessary suffering caused by false information and misconceptions around grief, which lead to self-criticism. So get curious instead!

2. Community

When you think you are alone in your struggle, it's easy to fall prey to a victim mindset. You start to believe that terrible things only happen to you. You wonder how you can possibly move forward. You think this loss has taken everything from you. But when you open your eyes to other people's struggles, there is proof that you are not the only one. Others are suffering AND bouncing back! Your struggle gets normalized, your grief gets witnessed, and you find hope and inspiration in a connection to others who are navigating a path forward too.

3. Coping Skills

Grief is a natural response to a loss, but in the acute phases of the feelings and emotions that arise may feel foreign and at times unsafe, due to their intensity and variation. With time you build a grief tolerance. Like muscle memory, your body familiarizes itself with these feelings and emotions and can begin to ride the neverending waves of grief. But to build this muscle, you need coping skills! Real tools, modalities, and exercises to help you regulate your nervous system, to move the energy through, and to release it so that you can connect back to you . . . and heal.

4. Connection

One of the biggest misconceptions around grief is that you need to "let go", or disconnect from your deceased loved one. This concept causes more suffering, because it asks you to cut emotional ties with your person in addition to the physical absence you're already grieving. Part of the work of integrating your loss is finding ways to maintain a connection to your loved one. Through prayer, by looking for signs, through song lyrics or in nature—or by my favorite, through the never-ending love that you have for him or her—you can maintain a connection far beyond the physical.

5. Compassion

Compassion goes a long way in grief. As I mentioned earlier, grievers are extremely hard on themselves, but if you can take a step back and become the observer of your situation, if you can really see everything that you are having to navigate and walk yourself through as you learn to cope with grief and adapt to daily life without your person, you may find it easier to give yourself a break. Grief is slow work, and rebuilding an entire life takes time. Grace and compassion allow you to ease in and make peace with the process.

6. Consciousness

A life-altering loss breaks you wide open! It's within the rupture that you are invited deep within to explore old wounds, conditioning, and trauma that have shaped you into who you are and how you see the world today. Sometimes it's hard and painful to look at these experiences, and often they stir up more grief. But as you reach new levels of consciousness within your healing journey, you become able to separate old wounds from the current grief, making it feel possible to navigate in the present; and access clarity around who you are at your core—your essence, your truth, and who you want to become.

Part One

Frozen

❧

*Sometimes grief gets frozen
within you. Like a cottage
in a frozen forest encrusted in ice,
so is your heart. With time,
the ice begins to thaw.
Your frozen heart melts.
You begin to feel.*

I opened my eyes and looked up at the vast sky through the warm, glassy, aquamarine water. Submerged, floating somewhere in time and space, I started to question—is this all a dream?

Less than three hours ago, my thirty-two-year-old husband passed away after a fifteen-month battle against cancer. My aunt had woken me up just as the sun was rising to tell me the news that Ian had died. I raced into the back room of the beach house that had been donated to us by a real-life guardian angel, to see the corpse of my once-healthy, vibrant, and very alive husband lying there. Lifeless.

Despite him already being gone, I embraced the shell of my husband and said my final goodbye. The hospice nurse had warned me the night before of his imminent passing, but his departure still didn't seem real. I couldn't process his death in that moment, and, honestly, I don't think I even cried.

My three-year-old awoke soon after and immediately my attention shifted from my dead husband to making her breakfast. As much as I wanted to ignore the real fact that her father was lying there, lifeless, just down the hallway and go pour Cheerios, I decided to kneel, look Izzy straight in the eyes, hold her body, and tell her the words that no mother ever wants to tell a child . . .

"Izzy, Daddy died."

She looked at me, reflecting my own disbelief and confusion, clearly not processing a word I had said. I continued.

"The cancer made Daddy's body stop working. He died and he's not going to be able to play or talk to us anymore. You also won't be able to see him much longer. Would you like to say goodbye?"

She shook her head. No. So I poured her a bowl of Cheerios and we went outside. After a few bites of breakfast, curiosity changed her mind. We slowly walked to the back room where Izzy stood next to her dead daddy—her shoulders just reaching the top of the hospital bed. She gently touched Ian's arm and quietly said, "Goodbye, Daddy." Then we walked out of the room and went to the beach.

The day of Ian's death felt like a normal day overall. The kids played in the sand, I swam in the ocean, and meanwhile my husband—their father—was taken away to the morgue. It felt like I was living in two alternate realties—one of crystalline water and kids laughing; and another of stale hospital beds and an empty corpse. My mind couldn't integrate it all.

The most important person in my life—my husband, the father of my children, my lover, best friend, and soulmate—was gone! And somehow, I was still here without him. I couldn't comprehend it.

The weeks and months that followed felt surreal. I was detached from this new reality that I was living in, and numb to feelings and emotion. The looks of pain and anguish from friends and family who visited us led me to believe that something was wrong with me. For my husband just passing away, I was holding up well . . . too well, perhaps?!

My world had completely stopped. But the outside world kept turning—phone calls to and from my husband's employer, paying medical bills, decisions about his memorial, and not to mention keeping a one- and a three-year-old alive. I somehow fulfilled these duties and demands, but my mind, heart, and body felt completely detached. They were somewhere else completely . . . beyond the sunrise, with Ian, in a realm too mysterious and vague to comprehend, I suppose.

I tried to slow down reality. I struggled to catch my breath. I literally could not process the magnitude of what had just happened! I turned to nature—finding solace hiking up ridges, feeling my feet in the dirt, and allowing the ocean breeze to tantalize all my senses to remind me that I was actually here, that this was in fact reality. I turned to yoga—seeking relief from the relentless chaos of the logistics of death, by grounding down into the earth with my hips planted on my mat, connecting to my breath, and tuning in to the moment.

Despite best efforts from friends and family, they just couldn't relate. This left me feeling desperately alone. In some ways I craved the isolation—being able to dive into my cocoon and protect myself from the reality of my new life. Where I could catch my breath, process, and try to feel.

At night I felt so alone. The side of the bed where Ian slept was being occupied by my three-year-old daughter, who couldn't sleep alone after Daddy left. After we returned from the beach on the day of Ian's death, she ran back into the house to find Daddy, but was met with an empty room.

"Where did Daddy go?" she asked me in disbelief.

Friends and family had already taken Ian's body to the morgue for cremation and hospice workers had cleaned out the medical equipment. Stumbling over my words I answered,

"He went to the sky! He's in the stars, the wind, the sun, and the moon."

"Like, POOF?!" Izzy questioned, glancing up and gesturing playfully.

"Kind of," I replied, in exhaustion.

Months after his death and celebration of life, I rocked in a hammock overlooking the islands where Ian's ashes were spread and thought to myself, I must be the only thirty-two-year-old widow out here. What am I going to do with my life? How am I going to raise two kids without my husband? Where do I even start?

When I looked to the future, I felt fear and paralysis. When I turned to the past, I felt pain and disbelief. So I focused on the now. After fighting cancer for almost two years, my new direction and purpose was simply to focus on the next best thing—to make it through one day, one hour, and one breath at a time.

Ian passed away in his home state of Hawaii. On the island I felt safe. With his ashes scattered in the ocean waters that I could hear, feel, and smell from my window, Ian felt close. I didn't want to return to our life in Colorado without him. But within three months, after a failed attempt to buy ice cream for my kids due to our joint credit cards being canceled, I could not avoid the return.

I had to reenter reality. And when I did, it hit hard.

My Person Died. Now What?

There is absolutely nothing that can prepare you for a loved one's death. Whether the loss was anticipated or sudden, it takes time, intentional healing, learning to calm your nervous system and ride the waves of emotions of grief for your brain, body, and heart to adapt and make sense of this massive change that has altered your life forever.

So slow down.

Despite the pace and demands of the outside world, there is no urgency to "be done" with this process. **Grief work is slow.** It's messy and unpredictable. It's not logical, it's non-linear, and often makes no sense at all.

Grief looks different for everyone, and whatever you are feeling is right! Read that again, because this is a hard but important truth to embrace—and I know because I've walked myself through the loads of the self-doubt and shattering of self-confidence that comes with a life-altering loss. I've witnessed clients create additional suffering, wondering if their grief was normal, or criticizing themselves for not grieving *right*.

Although grief is a universal experience, the way in which each unique individual grieves is not universal. It's highly personal, nuanced, and dependent upon the conditioning and past experiences that formed you long before your person's death. We will unearth this more in Part Five, but for now, I simply invite you to trust yourself. Trust that your emotions are valid, that you know deep down what you need, or what may feel supportive as you navigate this path. And if this feels like a stretch, trust that you aren't alone. It's extremely hard for grievers to trust themselves in this process, which is why I created this book.

I hope that the following pages serve not as a guide on how to do grief, but how **you can become your own best guide** through it.

Is This Normal?

Grief looks different for everyone and nothing prepares you for it.

When Ian passed away, I dissociated. Dissociation is a trauma response where your mind shuts off as a means to cope with too much stress. At the time I didn't know it, but the lack of emotion that I was feeling shortly after his passing (and in the several months that followed) was my brain protecting itself. I was criticizing myself for not being sad enough or feeling anything at all, when in fact I was in shock.

Another trauma response is dysregulation—where you get so flooded by your emotions that you struggle to control or regulate them.

If you feel totally lost in a fog, overwhelmed to the point of paralysis, or you can't get off the kitchen floor because you're crying so hard, please know that it's totally normal. Your brain is trying to process the impossible and it's going to take time—a lifetime, perhaps.

For now, I invite you again to **slow down.**

Gently turn inward and notice the thoughts that are swirling in your head; the questioning about whether how you are grieving is "right" or "wrong," "good" or "bad," or "normal"—because **just about every crazy thing you feel or do after a loved one's death is perfectly normal in grief!** Give yourself permission to feel and do it all.

"Crazy" Things You Experience in Grief

Here's list of all the "crazy" things that are not all that crazy after a loss, and that you could be experiencing as part of your grief right now.

If you're having other experiences in grief that aren't listed here, don't worry, this is just an overview. And if you're still concerned whether your thoughts, feelings, or behaviors are normal, talk to a grief-informed therapist, coach, or another griever. Someone has felt the same way that you are feeling.

Foggy brain: Feeling totally disoriented, you can't remember a thing, you're pouring orange juice into the cereal bowl, and your brain feels heavy.

Searching/yearning for your person: You try to call them on the phone, you wait for them to walk through the door, you wonder where they went. Other people may even start to look like them!

Appetite changes: Food may feel unappetizing or you may overeat; sometimes you eat but you can't taste anything at all.

Time distortion: You may not know what day or time it is. I mean, time stopped when your person died—*remind me why time matters anymore?*

Ruminating: Your brain is trying to make sense of the tsunami wave that just destroyed your entire life, so often thoughts get stuck processing the events of the death. It's figuring out the story, so to speak.

Asking yourself why?: This is the other part of the processing piece—searching for a reason or meaning in your loved one's death. (We will cover this more in Part Three!)

Playing the blame game: *Was it the doctor who missed a symptom? Was it me? If only I didn't let him get in the car? Was it God's fault?* The questioning and blame game are just your brain trying to find cause or a reason behind your person's death.

Emotional overwhelm: Experiencing uncontrollable crying, panic attacks, constant anxiety, bursts of anger and rage—feels like you are "drowning in your emotions," or you believe that the pain will kill you. (Tip: It won't!)

Feeling detached: Feeling numb and unable to emote. Life feels surreal.

Craving isolation: The outside world may feel fast, noisy, and too vibrant. You may find safety and comfort spending time alone.

Craving connection: Being alone may amplify the void and force you into your grief. You may not be ready for this, so connecting with others feels safe.

"Crazy" Things We Do in Grief

Here's a list of all the "crazy" things you may be doing in grief and judging yourself for, but, again, all these are *totally normal!* Again, this list is not comprehensive, but it gives you an idea of how different grief can look for everyone and how people cope in different ways.

- Wearing your dead person's clothing or wrapping yourself up in their favorite blanket.
- Talking to them out loud like they are still alive.
- Sobbing alone in your car as you listen to music that reminds you of them.
- Wanting to get rid of all of their belongings, then freaking out at the thought of not having them.
- Keeping transitional objects, like their jewelry, golf clubs, or favorite hat, or having their clothing made into a pillow or another item to bring you comfort.
- Going on shopping sprees to fill your closet instead of trying to fill the void in your heart.
- Working out so much that the physical pain hurts more than the emotional.
- Lying in bed all day because the weight of all you're carrying makes it feel impossible to move your body.
- Cocooning yourself in your house away from noise, happy people, and reality.
- Grabbing drinks with friends to drink (not advised) and laugh (advised) the pain away.
- Scrolling on social media for hours on end.
- Getting super into your work to distract from your grief—maybe even getting a promotion (this happens more than you'd think)!
- Not wanting to work at all because your perception of work or any career is forever jaded.

Why You Feel This Way

Let's dive into these different responses by breaking down the common feelings and emotions that are experienced in grief.

Like I said, I totally judged myself for not being sad after my husband's death. But at a very biological and nervous system level, my body was just in shock. I was having a trauma response—meaning I was unable to control my feelings and emotions during that time.

Once I learned that I was in shock and that this response was totally normal, I felt relief and released the judgment I was holding around how I was grieving. I reduced the amount of suffering I was enduring, too.

Grief *is* a natural and normal *response* to a loss. Due to the intensity and range of feelings and emotions that arise in the grieving process, the experience can feel overwhelming and confusing. After a loss . . .

- You may feel like you are drowning in your emotions.
- You may feel nothing at all.
- You may feel disoriented, foggy-brained, and totally lost.
- You may feel like you are downright losing your mind!

These are all *normal* responses to a loss and a sign of your brain and body trying to process the magnitude of the tragedy that just occurred in your life. There is nothing wrong with you!

So instead of criticizing yourself for feeling this way, I invite you to get curious about your grief and learn about the common feelings and emotions that arise after a loss.

Shock and Denial

Shock and denial are often felt during or shortly after a loss. These feelings come up due to your body and your brain's inability to process and accept that something terrible has happened to you.

Sometimes your heart needs more time
to accept what your heart already knows. —Paulo Coelho

These feelings are essentially defenses trying to protect you from the pain, and they may manifest as:

- fatigue
- lack of motivation
- numbness
- disbelief
- sleeplessness and vivid dreams
- feeling paralyzed
- irritability

. . . among other sensations.

Life doesn't feel real; it doesn't make sense; and it can feel totally meaningless. While numbness can be confused with "not caring," this sensation is your body trying to protect itself from the pain.

The same goes with denial. "Denial" can be a triggering word (because you are fully aware that something tragic and awful just happened to you!), yet denial is actually just our mind trying to catch up and process everything that occurred. Think of denial as your body's natural "shock absorber."

Shock and denial work together to protect you from the pain, only allowing in what we are ready to handle.

Anxiety

Anxiety is often overlooked as part of grief, but it's actually incredibly common! When your entire world implodes on you, it's normal to feel overwhelmed, worried, or apprehensive about another tragedy lurking around the corner, and feel tense navigating a foreign environment without your loved one in it.

Anxiety occurs in relation to stress, which is a physiological and psychological response to a real or perceived threat. After a loss, everything is foreign and new, so your body perceives this as a highly threatening landscape.

There are several factors that contribute to anxiety after a loss:

- The intense and varied emotions brought on by grief.
- How your body and mind are learning to embrace and cope with these changes.
- The threat to your own mortality and future losses.
- Logistical issues, like managing finances and the deceased's belongings or estate, etc.
- Supporting other family members' grief.
- Unresolved issues or fear of forgetting your person.
- Unprocessed grief and past trauma.

When you're confronted with a threat, your sympathetic nervous system stimulates the adrenal glands, causing them to release hormones like adrenaline and cortisol as part of our body's natural fight-or-flight response.

Emotionally, you may feel tense, jumpy, restless, irritable, and sometimes you might start anticipating the worst. Physically, you may experience a racing heart, shortness of breath, sleeplessness, and headaches, among other sensations.

If you've been feeling *on edge*, fearful of another tragedy occurring, and overwhelmed since your loved one died, this is WHY! You are going through a lot. Anxiety is your body naturally responding to this massive loss—i.e., a perceived threat—in your life.

Sadness

Sadness is one of the most natural, expected, and universal responses to grief and loss. When you love someone deeply and then lose them, it hurts. To be *bereaved* literally means to be "torn apart," and that pain you feel is sadness.

In your body, sadness can feel like emptiness, despair, heaviness, yearning, or even deep loneliness. Sadness can also result in high stress and can even affect your immune system and appetite.

Sadness is outwardly expressed through tears, but fear may prevent you crying. Often, grievers suppress their tears out of fear of not belonging or not behaving within societal norms, or because they worry that the tears will never stop. The tears *will* stop, and crying is how you feel and release sadness. While crying is one form of sadness, you can still feel sad without tears.

Sadness can manifest as heaviness, fatigue, apathy, and even depression— which is actually an appropriate response to a great loss. It's natural to withdraw from life when you are in the intense fog, disorientation, and processing of life after loss.

*While depression is expected, if you can't break the cycle the possibility of suffering a clinical depression should be addressed and you should consult a medical professional.

The more you hurt. The more you've loved.

Guilt

Guilt and grief go hand in hand. When someone leaves you before you are ready to say goodbye, there will always be unresolved questions or things unsaid or done that you wish you could have achieved when your person was alive.

You may have regrets, self-blame, and thoughts about what you *should have, would have* or *could have* done differently surrounding your loved one's death. Many times, you fail to recognize that this degree of clarity can only be achieved in hindsight.

Guilt stems from your desire to rectify your last moments with your person, it can keep you stuck in the past, and it can prevent you moving through other emotions experienced in grief.

COMMON TYPES OF GUILT

Survivor's guilt: When survivors feel guilty that they survived when others died. They may believe they could have done something more to save the life of a person. They may ruminate about the loss and experience regret. Sometimes people experiencing survivor's guilt feel that they should have died rather than the deceased.

Guilt over moving forward too quickly: This may happen when you feel happiness, joy, or excitement about life after a loved one dies. You feel guilty for feeling good or moving forward with life, because your mind convinces you that you are abandoning the deceased if you aren't feeling pain.

Guilt that you could/would/should have done something differently: Feelings of guilt manifest as regrets and they arise when you wish that we could have done things differently. In hindsight it feels like there was always more time that you could have spent with your person, or more things that we could have said. Regrets naturally arise when someone leaves before their anticipated time.

There is healthy guilt—meaning you actually did something wrong; and there's unhealthy guilt—which is a story you are creating.

As you search for a "reason" behind your person's death, you may find yourself linking events together that "caused" their death. This is called proximal causation, which is when you believe that an event—such as a call, argument, what the deceased ate—resulted in your person's death.

It's okay if you are thinking this way! This is your mind trying to process and make meaning of your person's death. What we will explore in later chapters is that there often is no reason behind someone's death. Death is random.

But as meaning-makers, your brain tries to find a reason. It struggles to accept that the world is random and uncertain. It creates stories, choosing to feel guilty rather than powerless.

Guilt is valid; and it needs to be processed and challenged to be released.

Anger

Anger is another normal response to a loss, but it's an emotion that is so hard for grievers to embrace. Society has demonized anger and categorized it as an inappropriate emotional response, but after a loved one's death you have a right to feel angry!

Just like other common emotions and feelings experienced during the grieving process, anger is your body's natural response to a perceived or real threat.

Death is a threat. Death is a reminder of your own mortality, and that the world is not a safe and predictable place. Not only that, but death also isn't fair— especially when it comes to someone you love. It feels like you got cheated or served an injustice. *Why me? Why my person?* This isn't fair! Losing someone also causes heartbreak and pain, which nobody wants to feel. Of course, anger arises when you feel hurt.

Think of the kid who gets pushed down on the playground and retaliates with anger—maybe name-calling or even a push back. Beneath that anger is hurt. There is pain and sadness. Anger is sadness's defense.

On a physiological level, anger triggers your body's fight-or-flight response. This causes your body to release adrenaline, your muscles to tighten, your heart rate and blood pressure to increase, and your body's temperature to rise.

If anger isn't addressed, this constant flood of stress chemicals can actually lead to short- and long-term health problems such as headaches, digestion problems, depression, and anxiety.

Anger is an emotion, which can be felt without a thought attached to it—you can feel anger in your body even without being consciously aware of the root cause. If you have an outburst of anger that seemingly came out of nowhere, there is an underlying reason.

It's okay to feel anger—pure rage—that your person is no longer here. The best thing that you can do for yourself right now is to acknowledge this feeling . . . otherwise it just speaks louder. We will cover some coping skills and ways to move through anger in Part Two.

Loneliness

Loneliness is your body's natural response to fear. Human beings are wired for connection. When you lose someone you love, you also lose that connection to them. Seemingly simple, mundane, everyday tasks like picking up your phone to call someone and not having your loved one to answer, can trigger feelings of loneliness.

This happens because your nervous system is responding to the change in your external environment—of taking up physical space alone. It can feel like actual hollowness, and sometimes you can even feel out of control, paralyzed, or spiraling. This can be attributed to fear and your body's natural fight-or-flight response.

It's important to understand that loneliness is a feeling—meaning it's a physiological response to a THOUGHT. This is important to recognize because YOUR THOUGHTS PLAY A MAJOR ROLE IN HOW YOU FEEL.

Individual loneliness is defined by what you WANT versus what you HAVE— which will look different for everyone. You may feel lonely because you WANT your person but what you HAVE is a void. You may feel lonely because you WANT others to understand you but what you HAVE is judgment and criticism.

In grief, sometimes it feels safe or comforting to be alone—away from the pace of the outside world, where you can slow down and process your thoughts. In this instance, the feelings about being physically alone would be defined as solitude, whereas in other scenarios you may crave connection and when you don't have it, the resulting feeling is loneliness.

Loneliness is the poverty of self; solitude is the richness of self.
Loneliness expresses the pain of being alone;
solitude expresses the glory of being alone. —May Sarton

I hope that learning about your emotions and feelings helps you to normalize them and gets you one step closer to trusting in yourself. If you start to criticize yourself for feeling a certain way, instead get curious about your emotions. They are all valid, thus they are all worth being felt.

Turn your criticism into curiosity.

There is nothing wrong with you . . . this is just grief. If you are looking for ways to cope with these feelings, skip to Part Two. For now, simply trust that what you are feeling . . . is right.

Becoming Your Own Grief Guide

Remember, nothing has prepared you for this loss. Your person died without your consent. And there is no right or wrong way to do grief—there are no true rules or guides. What I'm sharing with you in the pages of this book is how to be your own best guide . . .

- By trusting yourself.
- By giving yourself permission.
- By honoring all of your feelings and emotions.
- By breaking down harmful misconceptions around grief that will ultimately add to your suffering.

When Ian died, I thought I should be totally wrecked, wailing away in devastation, lying in bed for days, sobbing on the bathroom floor, and questioning how I could possibly go on with my life. When I found myself doing okay—because of my body's beautiful protective layer of shock—I immediately judged myself.

I had never experienced a close loss like this. The only understanding of grief that I had was a dramatized version of what I had seen in the movies. I also largely relied on input from my friends and family members, hearing advice which, despite being well-*intentioned,* was not well-*informed:* "Just stay busy." "Don't talk about the death with your kids." "You've got to move on." "He would want you to be happy." "You're young . . . you'll find another husband."

You will not 'get over' the loss of a loved one; you will learn to live with it.
You will heal and you will rebuild yourself around the loss you have suffered.
You will be whole again, but you will never be the same.
Nor should you be the same, nor would you want to.

—Elisabeth Kübler-Ross

It was then that getting curious about grief and how this all was *really* supposed to go down helped me to separate truly supportive advice from the misconceptions that our society largely draws upon when trying to support someone in grief.

So, let's break down some of these common misconceptions.

Time Frame for Grief

The time frame for grief probably surprised me most! *Is there no end to this?* I struggled to comprehend.

I see many grievers hit their first-year death anniversary and wonder why they don't feel differently. They beat themselves up for "regressing" when their emotions are often more intense in the second year due to the shock finally lifting, and their unrealistic expectation that *their grief should be done* only adds suffering to the already painful process.

Like I said, grief work is slow. It takes a lifetime to integrate the loss of a loved one, because grief is the price you pay for love.

GRIEF MYTHS

There is only one way to grieve. Some grievers feel sadness immediately after a loss, while some don't experience sorrow for a year. Some experience rage and fury, while others may not feel anger at all. Some people grieve through busying themselves, while others lie in bed for days. This is because each person's grief journey is highly unique. Grief looks different for everyone. Remember this when you find yourself comparing your grief to others who are grieving the same loss (potential family and friends), or different ones (i.e., on social media). There is no wrong, right, or one way to grieve.

Grief is linear and is experienced in stages. Grief is a messy, complicated path that unfolds in layers upon layers and ebbs and flows like the ocean tide. There is no formal progression of grief; you don't finish one stage and then move on to the next. Feelings are fluid—they come and they go—and it's much easier to ride the neverending, ever-changing current when you embrace this truth.

Grief has an endpoint. Believing that grief has an endpoint will set you up for failure and disappointment. There is no "finish line" with grief. You are never done! Grief doesn't ever really go away, but it does change. It can be years after a loss and grief may still arise. There is nothing wrong with you! You are not regressing. This is just the price you pay for love.

Ignoring the pain will make it go away. Suppressing or avoiding the hard emotions in grief does not make them go away. Instead, this energy can get stuck in your body and cause psychological, emotional, and physiological problems. You can't heal what you don't feel. You integrate your loss by processing and feeling your emotions.

If you are happy, then you must be finished grieving. Grief and joy coexist. After a loss, you can be happy, hurt, and healing simultaneously. Feelings are fluid! A griever may be smiling one moment and then crying the next. Integrating requires tending to your grief as you adapt to your new normal. Healing is about learning to live alongside your grief.

> **The first year is the hardest.** It's different for everyone. Most grievers are led to believe that if they survive the first year of grief, then they will be done. Depending on the type of loss and griever, many find that the second, third, or consecutive years after are harder, as the shock lifts and the permanence of their loss settles in.
>
> **You will feel normal again.** A life-altering loss changes the very fabric of who you are. A piece of you has died with your person and has to be grieved and reborn as the integrated version of you. A you who knows loss, pain, and suffering, and the growth, light, meaning, and potential on the other side. There is no normal to return to. You are forever changed.

One more time so you can hear me in the back row: slow down! Try not to rush this. We live in a society that moves really fast! Think about it—you order a package on the internet and it's literally outside your door the next day. We want quick results, logic, answers, and control, but after a life-altering loss these attributes are hard to come by. Grief takes time. It's messy and ultimately forces you to surrender to all that is outside of your control and learn to live in uncertainty.

So the sooner you can release the need to "finish" and rush the process, the sooner you will be able to drastically reduce the amount of suffering in grief.

You won't always feel pain and suffering. Your grief will change. And you will learn to live alongside your grief as the neverending love for your person. By letting go of timelines, dispelling harmful myths, and releasing any expectations around how you "should" grieve, you can tap into trust and allow your grief to guide you.

Though this will differ for everyone, here's a timeline for experiencing grief:

Anticipatory grief: Grief that occurs before the actual death.

Acute grief: Grief experienced shortly after the death (zero to nine months) where emotions may be more volatile, overwhelming, or you may feel nothing at all due to shock.

Early grief: Grief experienced in the first two years since the death. Emotions and feelings will look different for everyone.

Mature grief: Grief you experience for the rest of your life.

Stop "Should"ing Yourself

Often in grief, your mind creates a story that you *"should be further along by now"* or *"should be feeling something else"* instead of just embracing your grief. When you "should" on yourself, you end up getting caught in the cycle of negative thought.

The negative thoughts and stories about your grief are what create the unnecessary suffering. The pain is necessary. It's part of the process. It's the emotion behind the emotions that adds to your suffering.

So, are you starting to see how getting curious about grief can help validate and normalize your experience?

Take a deep breath. This is a lot.

The weight of the magnitude of this loss feels impossible to carry; and the fear of the future—of rebuilding your life without your loved one in it—feels overwhelming and at times paralyzing. So here is my invitation to take this journey one step at a time. The nightmare has already happened and you are still here. Yes, it feels like a dream, but unbelievably you have already survived the worst of it.

Life moving forward is a big question mark. It's unsettling to not have all of the answers, but I promise they will come. For now, can you perhaps make peace with uncertainty by bringing the timeline closer and focusing on the next right thing?

Again, slow down. Healing takes time.

Toolkit for Acute Grief

These are some basic ways that you can support yourself right now as you cope with grief and begin to feel the pain and reality of this massive void

A NOTE ON SUDDEN LOSS VS. ANTICIPATED LOSS

Whether it's a sudden loss or anticipated one, nothing can prepare you for the death of a loved one and the grief that follows. Grief expert David Kessler says that, "with sudden loss, you dive in and with anticipated you wade in, but despite how we get there we all end up in the same ocean of grief."

This is so true, and both types of losses present different challenges and complexities. There is no need to qualify or compare which type is harder or worse, but just to shine light on some subtle differences:

Grief from sudden losses may be more traumatic. Because trauma is subjective to each person's experience, anticipated losses can be traumatic as well. If you find yourself experiencing flashbacks, ruminating in the story of your person's death, having panic attacks because your nervous system believes it's reliving the day of the death, you may consider consulting a trauma-informed therapist or coach to help you cope. Separating grief from trauma facilitates healing and ensures you receive the proper type of support.

Those who suffer a sudden loss may experience a higher degree of shock and denial following a loved one's death, because it's more difficult for your brain to process and integrate this drastic change in such a quick time. You may question why you aren't feeling anything or why you are seemingly doing "okay"—this is why! You are in shock.

With anticipated loss, your grief journey starts from the day of your person's diagnosis—meaning you are already grieving them before their actual death. Sometimes this gives grievers the misconception that they should be more prepared for their person's passing, resulting in guilt and regret. Grievers who have been caretaking for a long time may feel like they have lost their sense of purpose, or they may even feel a sense of relief to no longer see their person in pain and be able to return to everyday duties and life. Often, grievers who have experienced anticipated loss have to re-process the anticipatory grief that they bypassed in survival mode while trying to keep their person alive.

in your life. These tips reduce unnecessary suffering, build resilience, and strengthen your "grief muscle" as you learn to ride the waves and will help you to support yourself in the early months to the first year following a loved one's death:

- Slow down! I said it again. But really, I mean it.
- Remind yourself that not everything has to be done right away. Prioritize the "logistics of death" list (executing the will, planning the memorial, getting rid of belongings) and slowly—very slowly—cross items off.
- Ask for help with tackling the list or find someone to ask for help for you! Also enlist helpers for cooking, shopping, cleaning, or sprinkling joy into your life.
- Give yourself permission to feel it all.
- Trust that what you are feeling is "right"—all of your emotions are real, thus they are valid.
- Give yourself grace and honor in whatever you need to do right now.
- If you don't feel anything at all—it's okay—you are likely in shock (your body is protecting you from the pain).
- Slow down and rest—it may feel like you have to get back to "normal" but remember, there is no normal. You will rebuild your life one slow step at a time.
- Take as much time off from work or other duties as possible (even if this means finding someone to watch your kids).
- If you do have kids, put taking care of yourself first! Think of the oxygen mask on the airplane and put yours on before those of your kids so you can support them in the way they need to be supported.
- Explore ways to ground down and access safety within you—walk in nature, lie on the ground, take a gentle restorative yoga class.
- Nourish your body—eat food, drink water, sleep—these are all basic human needs that often get overlooked in acute grief.

- Explore ways to connect to your loved one in spirit.
- Get curious about grief and others' experience of loss—read memoirs, listen to podcasts, or follow similar losses on social media—anything that can help normalize your experience.
- Seek professional support by talking to a therapist or grief coach, or by joining a grief support group (online or in-person).
- Schedule in your joy! This may feel like a stretch right now, but write down a few things that make you smile and call a friend who will help you find these little joys with you.

The Power of Connection

Human beings are a social species. We are wired for connection! In fact, Maslow's Hierarchy of Needs ranks love and belonging among the most important needs besides food, water, and safety. Our desire for connection includes having interpersonal relationships, intimacy, and being integrated into a group. When these needs are met, our overall well-being improves and we live a more fulfilled life.

After a loss, the basic human need of connection vastly changes. Not only do you lose your person, but you lose simple moments like calling them on the phone, making decisions together, and dreaming about the future. You lose pieces of yourself—your identity and purpose as well as your role as friend, mother, husband, or wife. Dynamics between friends and acquaintances and family structures change as well, when the person who used to be the "glue" that brought everyone together is no longer there.

These secondary losses—invisible losses that are only clear to the griever (I cover more of this in Part Two) are just as painful as the primary loss and leave a massive void in the basic human need of connection.

So, what do you do to fill this void?

You grieve these losses . . . AND you adapt. You find *new ways* to maintain the connection.

Moving On vs. Moving Forward

In grief, words really matter. After a life-altering loss, you really move *on*. Why? Because *moving on* implies letting go or disconnecting from your loved one.

After a loss, you move *forward*. Moving forward touches on the concept of integration by acknowledging that this loss will change you forever. Your grief will shape you into the person you are becoming, and the more you accept this, the easier it becomes to see that your deceased loved one still plays a major impact in your life—no, not in the physical, but in his or her absence.

Your deceased loved one becomes woven into every part of who you are and what you do in life as you move forward without them.

Society holds the misconception around grief that you need to "let go" or disconnect from a deceased loved one in order to carry on with life. Upon further research, this belief dates back to the 1917 paper "Mourning and Melancholia," written by Sigmund Freud, where he explains that grievers must relinquish attachments to and break bonds with deceased love in order to move on with life.

What modern grief counseling teaches is that *letting go, forgetting about* or disconnecting emotionally from your deceased loved one actually creates more suffering!

Healing—or integration—is about weaving the **entire experience of loss** (even the painful parts) into your life as you move forward. This process of integration is multi-faceted, but one essential component is finding ways to maintain a lasting connection to your deceased loved one. Connecting to your loved one "in spirit," through love or in gratitude for the time you had together, doesn't take away the pain of losing them in the physical world, but it softens it.

Tools to Maintain a Connection to Your Deceased

You can carry your person and your love for them *with* you, as you move forward! Here are some ways to do this.

- Write a letter to them telling them how much you miss them or what life is like without them.

- Light a candle and have a moment of silence as you feel your emotions.

- Listen to music that reminds you of them and makes you think of them speaking to you through the lyrics.

- Look at pictures or videos of the times you shared together.

- Talk about them!

- Visit places that remind you of them or take a trip you wanted to take together.

- Honor them on birthdays, holidays, or other milestones you wish they could be a part of.

- Explore talking to a medium—a psychic who can connect with the spirit world.

- Adopt a hobby they enjoyed.

- Adopt a transitional object—keep your loved one's clothing, picture, or jewelry close to bring you comfort.

- Look for signs.

- Pray.

Connection to Communities

Another thought that crossed my mind shortly after Ian's death was that I genuinely believed that I was the only thirty-two-year-old widow out there! I knew of one other young widow in my immediate circle of friends, but besides her I felt so utterly alone.

What changed this belief and shifted me out of a victim mindset—thinking that it was *only me* whose situation was so dire—was connecting with other widows! I talked to my one widow friend, I joined groups on social media for young widows, and I searched the hashtag #youngwidow and found hundreds of widows talking about their experience of loss. I realized that I wasn't the only thirty-two-year-old widow and there was a community out there who got me! I hated this new club, but at the same time I was so grateful for it.

Belonging and interpersonal relationships satisfy our basic human need for connection. But after a loss, grievers are often met with misunderstanding and disconnect. Friends and family who have wonderful intentions may say the wrong things or give harmful advice because they don't understand the experience of grief and loss.

You may look to friends or family for validation or permission to feel or act in a certain way, and in return you get judgment or criticism. You may seek a shoulder to cry on or someone to simply listen, and instead receive platitudes or silver linings that, while well-intentioned, feel like they minimize your experience of loss.

This lack of collective understanding, compassion, or empathy often leads grievers to believe that their grief is a burden or a problem to be solved or "fixed." Unfortunately, most people don't know how to hold space or be with someone facing profound tragedy. Your grief may make others feel uncomfortable because of this.

This is not your fault!

This is a hard reality to exist within and can feel deeply hurtful, especially in the initial stages of grief when emotions are already high and you're feeling unsure about how to navigate a path forward.

This is why finding a community who understands is so important to the grieving process! When you join a group of like-minded people navigating similar experiences there is immediate connection. Without even expressing words, observing others who are also walking the path of grief and loss forms a visceral bond.

Instead of platitudes and affirmations to "make you feel better," you get a glimpse of hope by watching others rise from the ashes and begin to believe that if she can—I can too!

Goodbyes are only for those who love with their eyes. Because for those who love with heart and soul there is no such thing as separation. —Rumi

You break down the walls of isolation and comparison that trap you in victim mindset because you realize that others are also struggling.

You release self-doubt and silence the voices in your head wondering *is this normal?*, because you realize that others feel the same as you do.

Your feelings are held. Not judged.

Your experience gets normalized. Not stigmatized.

Your struggle gets validated. Not pitied.

Your grief gets witnessed. Not fixed.

As you journey through grief in community, you increase your access to a range of tips, tools, and wisdom from others! You take what supports you and you leave the rest. You begin to notice that what brings you healing and comfort may be totally different from somebody else and that this doesn't make your experience *wrong*—just different.

Because grief looks different for everyone! Yet, despite all the different ways to heal, grow, and find meaning in life after loss, for grievers there is one universal need: for grief to be witnessed!

The act of sharing your story of your loss, your grief, and your daily struggles of rebuilding your life without your person in a safe space, where these feelings can simply be held and acknowledged; allows the griever's experience to be fully seen.

Grievers need the outside world to witness what's happening on the inside. They need their experience to be recognized—to reflect back their truth that their deceased person, their loss, and their grief matters.

Grief can be witnessed in many ways—not just in physical, in-person grief groups. Now, you can jump on social media to share your loss and have your grief witnessed by followers who comment and like your posts. Keep in mind that when you share publicly on social media, anyone can engage with your posts. So consider maintaining privacy measures if you want to protect yourself from internet trolls or others who may leave negative comments and cause more pain.

To ensure that your grief gets witnessed in a supportive way and that you feel safe and secure enough to share, I recommend joining a community centered on grief and loss.

How to Find Your Community

In the modern world, there are so many ways to find your people! Here are some ideas to get you started.

Facebook groups: Once you find a person or organization to follow on social media, you can see if they have a Facebook group. These are often free and are an easy way to connect with other grievers.

Grief organizations/coaches: You can also search for organizations or coaches who hold online and in-person support groups. Here are some of my favorites:

- **All types of loss:** Tender Hearts—grief.com; move*THRU*—movethrugrief.com
- **Parent loss:** Motherless Daughters—hopeedelman.com; Dougy Center—dougy.org
- **Child loss:** The Compassionate Friends—compassionatefriends.org
- **Younger adults experiencing loss:** The Dinner Party—thedinnerparty.org

Connection to Yourself

Like I said, the journey through grief is ultimately about learning how to trust yourself again. But how do you access trust when this loss has rocked you to your core?

When you feel like you don't know who you are anymore.

When your hopes, dreams, and sense of purpose in life died with your person, and when the one person you want to talk to about it with isn't there to answer.

All your life you've been taught to look OUTSIDE of yourself for these answers . . .

What will make me happy? What will bring meaning and purpose to my life? Who am I destined to become?

But grief invites you to start this process WITHIN. In the darkness, in the disorientation, and in total despair.

If you are willing to accept this invitation, you can unlock new codes about yourself that allow you to embrace grief as love, to decrease your suffering, and to understand who you are and what you want in life moving forward.

This journey begins with learning to feel your emotions and tiptoe into the pain. The only path to grief is through it . . . so let's get moving.

And when great souls die, after a period peace blooms,
slowly and always irregularly. Spaces fill with a kind of soothing
electric vibration. Our senses, restored, never to be the same, whisper to us.
They existed. We can be. Be and be better. For they existed. —Maya Angelou

Part Two

Move

❧

The death of a loved one can make you feel powerless. The spiral of negative thoughts and weight of grief is almost paralyzing at times. When hope is hard to access through the lens of your mind, move your body! Movement reminds us of just how strong and capable we are.

There it was. Official and on paper. To all of society, the outside world, and the government in that moment my marriage was over. But to me, I still felt like Ian's wife! I knew that Ian was dead, but I wasn't ready to let go of my role as his wife.

I took a deep breath and finished the rest of the application as quickly as possible to beat the tears that were building within me.

In the stillness of my drive home, I felt a range of emotions. The official acknowledgment added a finality to Ian's death. My new widow status forced me into a new layer of acceptance around his passing. In Hawaii, I had still felt like I was dreaming—the shock had been protecting me. But now, the fog had lifted and reality was hitting hard.

I felt **anger**—why should a thirty-two-year-old, perfectly healthy man get cancer and die? I resented other happy, "full" families that had it better than me. Why did life treat us so unfairly?

I felt **anxiety**—how was I supposed to re-build an entire life? How could I raise two young kids on my own? What job paid enough and gave me the freedom to be a mom? And on top of all the logistics I was facing, I had my own grief to navigate.

I felt **lonely**—even though I had two young kids attached at the hip, I felt completely isolated in this new normal. Going to the grocery store, I looked fine on the surface but on the inside my heart was breaking. I didn't like how no one knew what was really happening within me! And to the people who knew my story of tragedy, I felt like they never could truly understand.

I felt **sad**—I missed Ian. My best friend and father of my kids. I didn't just miss him as a person but I grieved all of the roles that he played—my handyman, provider, father, shared decision maker, and life partner.

All of these pieces I had to grieve and feel simultaneously, while also keeping two young kids and myself alive.

I felt powerless living my new reality. Stuck, not really knowing how to carve out a path forward. Everything about the future seemed so vast and overwhelming—it was paralyzing at times.

But the one thing that helped me take back control in a life where I had lost it *was moving my body!*

Exercised helped me move through my emotions—feel them and release them—in a way that talk therapy could not. With every rep of a heavy weight, I felt not just physically stronger but also mentally and emotionally more capable. With every burst of cardio I felt a sense of freedom in a world where I was otherwise feeling trapped. And with every challenging workout accomplished, I felt a sense of optimism and hope.

Working out was proof that I was capable of stretching my capacity to do hard—sometimes unimaginable—things. And the pain I experienced in a physical workout gave me permission to feel my emotional pain. It reminded me that pain was part of the process, but the suffering was optional.

Fitness was no longer just about the physical reward of looking fit or supporting my health, it was a workout from the inside out! When I felt the resentment of being a solo mom of two brewing within me, I would call a babysitter and go to a HIIT class where I could throw punches and slam around weights.

When I felt sadness, I carried the weight of my grief in restorative yoga flow and cried lying in shavasana—corpse pose—as I thought of my dead husband lying there with me. The combination of hot, humid air and sweat masked my tears and I felt at peace just lying there in my sadness.

When I felt the crippling anxiety take over—the fears, doubts, and questions spiraling in my head—the overwhelm of the nightmare I was living, I slipped on my running shoes and hit the pavement. I could break the negative thought cycle, ground down with each stride, and quiet the noise in my mind as I connected to and focused on my heartbeat and breath.

Pain is inevitable. Suffering is optional. —Buddhist saying

I discovered that I could embody each unique emotion through movement—feel it—and when I was finished moving, I felt relief. Like I had literally moved the emotion through my body and released it!

Movement became my number one coping outlet for grief. It got me out of my head (the birthplace of fear and doubt) and into my body (the home for trust and intuition), breaking the negative thought cycles that made me feel stuck, and in turn gave me a sense of power, control, and hope in an otherwise hopeless situation.

I wasn't happy about my new normal by any means, but I was no longer frozen. The grief within me had started to thaw and I was finding ways to move through it!

Integrating Your Loss

My return home to Denver forced me to **accept** the reality that Ian was really gone. The experience at the social security office, residing in our house that was made for four and now only held three, and the struggles of solo parenting forced me to accept Ian's death. And in doing so, I had to move through several layers of grief and thus begin the process of integration.

Integration is about weaving the full experience of your loss into who you are and what you want out of life moving forward. It doesn't happen by denying your struggle, suppressing your grief, or slapping on a smile and pretending you are okay. It happens by accepting your person's death head-on and then figuring out ways to adapt to life without them.

Acceptance

Acceptance has been misconstrued as the final stage of grief, due to Elisabeth Kübler-Ross's popular work around the Five Stages of Grief. Her book *On Grief and Grieving* attempts to organize and familiarize you with common emotions experienced in grief, but according to David Kessler, her mentee and author of the book *Finding Meaning: The Sixth Stage of Grief,* she never intended the stages to be linear or to appear in any order. Acceptance actually comes in layers and at multiple points throughout your grief journey. For example, completing the social security application forced me to accept that my marriage by law was terminated, but I wasn't ready to accept that Ian was no longer my husband. I still felt deeply connected to him in that way, and I didn't take off my wedding ring for another four months.

Acceptance also doesn't mean that you are happy about the situation or even okay with it. It simply means that you are accepting the circumstance as part of your reality. You are no longer bargaining, in denial, or resisting your reality, but allowing yourself to be with it and at some point—adapt.

Acceptance is the foundation for moving forward and rebuilding a life after loss.

To get there, you have to move through the resistance (denial, anger, and sadness), release yourself from the stories (guilt and old wounds), and embrace a mindset to move forward.

Acceptance and integration go hand in hand as you grieve what *was* to step into what *is*. They both occur over a lifetime—making grief the lifelong journey it is. I'm always surprised by a new layer of grief that I encounter—like opening my heart up to love again after my husband's death and how the experience of dating invited me into layers of healing.

This is the work of healing! And as much as it truly is work, it's empowering to know that there are steps you can take to not just survive this experience, but truly thrive.

Here is some of the work that is involved in integration:

- Talking about your person, your day-to-day struggles without them in your life, and having your grief witnessed by others.
- Learning how to cope with your emotions and regulate your nervous systems to ride the never-ending ways of grief.
- Releasing the burden of guilt, by realizing that you are NOT in fact as powerful as you believe (no, you could not change the outcome of your person's death as much as you wish you could).

- Forgiving yourself for your regrets by trusting that this perspective could only be achieved in hindsight.

- Looking at old wounds that amplify your grief in the present and feel like resistance, being stuck or that "bad things only happen to you."

- Finding ways to maintain a connection to your deceased—through signs, music lyrics, nature, journaling, or prayer for life, or perhaps a revised belief system in the world to plant the seeds for meaning making and rewriting the narrative of your loss.

By believing that even in your person's physical absence he or she still influences you to this day, and by knowing your loved one, by doing life together, by loving them *and* losing them, your deceased person is forever a part of you!

Integration is weaving the entire experience of loss (even the painful parts) into your life as you move forward. You carry your person and your love for them *with* you and allow their physical absence to shape who you are and what you do in life moving forward!

The concept of integration is a relatively new approach to grief. In fact, past psychology focused on the idea of closure after a loss. The premise was that if you detached from your person and the painful feelings associated with their death, then you could move forward with life. And for decades this has been the approach to grief—to "let go," to "move on," or to disconnect from the world we knew and loved with our person in it.

This isn't the case! And in most cases trying to sever emotional ties with the deceased only adds to your suffering. So if friends and family try to offer advice—encouraging you to *move on* or *get over it*—they are probably leaning on outdated information. Remember that the griever (i.e., YOU) is your best guide for grief.

Grieving in a Grief-averse Society

We live in a happiness-obsessed society that avoids topics of hardship and largely denies us the experience of grief and loss. These societal beliefs shape our understanding of what our unique grief experience "should" look like, when in reality there is no right or wrong. The work we must do is to identify what stories, beliefs, and thoughts about grief are serving us, and more importantly **which ones are adding to our suffering.**

It's normal—and **expected**—to feel the pain of a loss (for months, even years after your loved one's death). But we live in a society that puts pressure on grievers to rush the process, finish grieving, and get back to life as usual by year one. As I discussed in "common misconceptions about grief" in Part One, grief doesn't work this way. You are never done and you are forever changed by the experience of this loss.

So if you find yourself beating yourself up for feeling "too sad" or wondering why you aren't further along, remember . . .

Your emotions are not "good" or "bad," or "right" or "wrong." They are all relevant!

Release the charge around your emotions and stop qualifying them.

When you feel "off" or experience extra "grief," instead of asking yourself *What's wrong with me?* change the question to: *Why am I feeling this way?*

Shift your self—criticism to curiosity!

Notice the language you use when you feel a big emotion. Often I hear clients say phrases like, *I'm such a mess* or *I just feel so weak!* when in reality it takes so much courage to feel the pain.

Remember that you are moving through the pain to access the love.

You might have already heard the common platitude—"insert your deceased loved one's name" *would want you to be happy!*

I heard it too after my husband died, and I would smile and think to myself—*Well, duh! Of course he would want me to eventually be happy, but I'm pretty sure he'd expect me to be sad that he died too.*

Pain Is Part of the Process. Suffering Is Optional.

As we covered in Part One, grief is a natural response to a loss. An essential part of the healing work, or integration, is to . . .

- Feel your feelings.
- Emote.
- Give your heart the space to grieve and process the magnitude of this tragedy so that eventually . . .

Remember your person with more love than pain.

You can't heal, what you don't feel. —David Kessler

Grief Is Love!

It's just underneath all the pain. So in order to get to the love, you have to move through the layers of pain.

In this section I'll provide you with coping strategies and movement exercises that give you a lifeline—relief—as you dip your toes into the pain to feel it, eventually alchemizing it as love.

So if grief is just a normal response to a loss and pain is *literally* part of the process . . .

Why is that we have such a hard time feeling our feelings?

Why do we criticize ourselves for feeling too sad or being unable to access happiness and joy after a loved one's death?

And why are we afraid to enter into the pain in the first place?

If this is you, don't worry! In addition to being biologically programmed to avoid pain, there are several other reasons why you tend to have emotions over your emotions—such as feeling ashamed for being angry, or feeling anxious when you can't stop crying.

There is actually a term for this: inhibitory emotions (which I'll discuss in a bit), but **the stories that you create around your experience of grief are what actually creates more suffering!**

My goal is to make you conscious of these thought patterns—the concerns, questions, self-doubt, and criticism—and help you understand where the originating belief is coming from; that so you can stop yourself in act and rewrite the pattern, in order to **prevent unnecessary suffering.**

Remember, the pain is part of the process (like a running a marathon or doing a hard workout). The suffering is optional.

Sources of Suffering

The main sources of suffering that I see in my clients are from:

- The stories he or she creates around the death and experience of loss.
- An inability to release the burden of guilt.
- Friends and family who don't understand (sad, but true).

So let's break these down a bit.

Your story of loss refers to the narrative you create around your loved one's death. For example, the facts of my loss were that Ian died at the age of thirty-two of uveal melanoma. But my story in the early months of grief was that this was my worst nightmare come true! My story was one of tragedy in darkness.

As I navigated grief and integrated my loss, Ian had still passed away from uveal melanoma at the age of thirty-two, but my story began to change. Instead of only tragedy and darkness, new themes like growth, survival, and resilience started to emerge.

The facts of the death stay the same. But the story changes. —Hope Edelman

I've learned that **I control the narrative** around my husband's death and my story continues to evolve with new chapters, including inspiration, new love, rebirth, and finding my soul's purpose.

Your ability to separate the facts of the death from the story is so important because it brings conscious awareness to the fact that you control the narrative! No, you cannot change the fact that your person died—and this realization comes with lots of painful emotions that you need to experience— but you can change the tragic trajectory moving forward. You can write the next chapter in a way that honors your deceased loved one and integrates them into your life, but you have to bring **conscious** awareness to the thought patterns that are telling you otherwise!

So let's explore what drives these thoughts.

What shapes your view of the world, specifically your perspective around death, grief, and struggle?

What factors make your life meaningful? Is it perpetual happiness and joy? Or is pain a part of it?

We will revisit these questions during Part Five, but for now, I invite you to do some digging with me as we explore your social conditioning, old wounds, and family upbringing to see how these factors might influence your present experience of loss.

Toolkit to Understand Old Stories

Your conditioning, old wounds, and family upbringing all inform your current experience of grief and loss. So I invite you to grab pen and paper or something to record yourself talking to reflect on the questions below.

Conditioning

Your brain is like a computer, and it absorbs information from the outside world like programming. You might not even know it because many of these beliefs are subconscious, but your perception of the world is largely influenced by these daily messages. Some common ones that I see influencing the grieving process are religious and cultural beliefs, and popular culture and entertainment.

- *How do my religious beliefs shape my perspective on death? Do I believe in an afterlife? Does God have a plan?*
- *How does my culture affect my experience of loss? What are the mourning rituals? What are the beliefs around death?*
- *How does popular culture and entertainment inform my perspective of death, grief, and loss? Do I feel like I should grieve in a certain way based on what I see in the media?*
- *How do these factors inform the way that I should or should not grieve?*

Old Wounds

Old wounds amplify grief in the present. Explore some of these questions to identify what an old wound feels like, and also to understand what needs to be healed in the past. (If you feel activated by digging into the past, it's best to seek professional counsel from a therapist to explore these questions.)

- *Do I feel like bad things always happen to me? Do I feel like I'm incapable of changing my situation?*
- *Does my grief feel familiar? Like I am starting to feel comfortable in the pain?*
- *What was my childhood like? Did I have a reliable mother/father figure? Or was I left to raise/support myself alone?*
- *Was either one of my parental figures a narcissist?* (If so, you might struggle to trust yourself and advocate for your needs.)
- *Do I have any past traumatic experiences, like previous losses, abuse, sexual assault, or abandonment?*

Family Upbringing

Your ability to flow with the darker emotions experienced in grief, as opposed to fight or suppress them, has a lot to do with how emotions were handled in your childhood. For example, you might feel like you need to cry but you *shame* yourself for doing because you were raised with the mentally that "boys don't cry."

- *How were emotions handled in my family? Did I feel safe to emote? Were feelings welcome?*
- *How was death or struggle handled? Was it talked about? Or kept private?*
- *Was I shamed or judged for feeling/behaving in certain ways?*
- *Did I feel safe to advocate for my needs? Why, or why not?*

Like I said, these influences are often subconscious, so a bit of digging is required to bring awareness to them! But once you do, you can separate the stories that are influencing your perception of death or of how you should grieve in order to choose which stories are serving you and which are not.

This is slow work that comes in layers, but I introduce it now because part of the healing work is to feel the pain. Unfortunately, I see several grievers blocking the pain, which adds more suffering, due to these stories.

Guilt

Another story that grievers might find themselves stuck in is one of guilt and regret. As discussed in Part One, guilt and regret commonly arise as your brain strives to search for a reason behind your loved one's death. It tries to link together events—creating a story about why your person died and how you could have altered the outcome. Here are some common examples to give you context:

- *If only I had seen the symptom sooner, then the cancer would not have spread.*
- *If only I had gotten him help earlier, then he would not have taken his life.*
- *If only I didn't let her get in the car, then she wouldn't have been killed by the drunk driver.*

If you have had similar thoughts about your person's death, don't worry—this is normal. Humans are meaning-making machines, and it's often easier for our brain to pinpoint a reason or name someone or something to blame instead of admitting that most death is random and out of our control.

What's important to recognize is that **guilt traps you in a story!** A story that may or may not be founded in truth, but in all cases blocks you from actually getting to feeling the pain of your loss—the grieving.

Toolkit to Release Guilt and Regret

Try these practices to challenge guilt or invite in compassion and forgiveness:

Make a list of all of your guilty thoughts:

For each one, ask yourself—Is this true? What moral code am I actually breaking?

If it is true, write a letter or record yourself asking your loved one for forgiveness.

If it's not true, try to challenge the guilty thought. For example . . .

Is it true that I don't deserve to be happy after my loved one died. Or is that just how I feel?

Can I say with 100 percent certainty that taking Ian to the doctor sooner would have changed the outcome of his survival? Or is that my mind trying to create a story?

Make a list of all of your regrets (the would-haves, should-haves, and could-haves):

Think about how you can't change the past and allow yourself to feel whatever comes up.

Write a letter (or record yourself talking) to your loved one asking for forgiveness—for all the things you would-have, should-have or could-have done when they were alive.

Then, write down the lesson in each regret—think of how this lesson might inform the way you move forward.

Create a list of commitments to yourself!

Write a letter (or record yourself talking) to your loved one telling them all of the things you wanted to say before he or she died.

Talk to a friend, family member, or therapist about your feelings of guilt. Often we need time to process the stories we are telling ourselves and assistance in challenging the parts that are untrue. Remember that friends and family might not be able to hold space for this type of work. Often guilt is illogical, but it's valid and friends and family might not understand this!

Affirmations to Release Guilt

There is nothing wrong with the way you are feeling. Be gentle with yourself as you slowly challenge your thoughts, release them with the following affirmations, and allow yourself to enter into the pain.

- I do not need to feel guilty anymore.
- I feel bad about some situations.
- It's okay to have these feelings.
- I do not need to blame myself.
- I did not know what I know now.
- Some things might be my fault, so I choose to change my behavior and learn from my mistakes.
- I cannot control 100 percent of situations.
- Not everything is my fault.
- I can feel bad about my situation AND accept it is not my fault.
- I release myself from feelings of guilt.

Friends and Family Who Don't Understand

The third source of additional suffering is friends and family who don't understand. These outside parties act as your mirror, reflecting back whether your grief looks normal, appropriate, too much, too slow, or too quick.

Because you've never experienced a loss of this magnitude, **it's hard to trust yourself.** You have a thousand voices in your head wondering *if you should be feeling a certain way* or *if this is normal.* Instead of listening to your own voice, you might find yourself looking to others for validation and support but end up being met with blank stares, unhelpful platitudes, or, even worse, more judgment and criticism.

This can feel heartbreaking on top of the grief you are already moving through, and incredibly isolating because it seems that there is literally no one else on the face of the earth who understands your circumstance. I get it, because I've been there too.

But at the same time, **it's not their fault!** (If you're rolling your eyes right now it's cool . . . like I said, I get it!)

It feels like they *should* understand, but I invite you to remember the version of yourself pre-loss.

- Would you have known how to support a griever?
- Did you have the right words?
- How would you have acted?

Your friends' and family's inability to support you is another product of living in a grief-averse society. Their desire to fix your grief and cheer you up is a systemic issue that permeates Western culture. You are a living reminder of their worst nightmare and their own mortality—and we all know that death is another topic our culture loves to avoid!

You have a right to feel upset and disappointed that others have let you down. But at the same time, can you hold compassion for the possibility that they just might not know how to act otherwise? In early grief, you might not be able to— and that's okay. I wasn't either!

You are surviving and you might not have room for compassion for anyone else but yourself. But with time and intentional healing, I invite you **to let go of the need for other's to understand your situation**—because, honestly, how could they?—and instead shift your perspective from needing others' permission or validation to source that from within.

You are your own best guide to grief! Only YOU truly know what you need. It's just really hard to trust yourself right now.

So here are some tips for how to deal with friends and family who don't get it, to help you to reduce the *external* noise and your *internal* suffering.

Toolkit for Dealing with Those Who Just Don't GET IT!

It's normal for friends and family to say the "wrong" thing or try to "fix" your pain instead of sit with you in it. Often they are trying to support you, but they truly don't know how. Remember, our society avoids topics like death, illness, grief, and loss like the plague—so YOU need to become your own best advocate. Despite knowing you well, friends and family can't read your mind! So as stretchy as it feels to ask for what you need, a little bit of communication can go a long way.

Here are some tips to guide the conversation:

Understand Your Needs

Ask yourself, *what do I need right now?* Is it someone to babysit my kids? To help me pack up my loved one's belongings? To assist with organizing finances? Some peace and quiet to grieve? No one knows what you need but YOU. So be honest with yourself and get really clear on what would feel supportive for you. Write it down and make a list. Then go out and ask for help!

Understand What You DON'T Need

This is arguably just as important as knowing what you do need. If platitudes like *your dead person would want you to be happy* or *at least you can have another husband or baby* don't feel supportive, then make note of it! If friends or family are drowning you with advice—*read this book, see this therapist, talk to this psychic medium*—when all you want to do is throw another grief book across the living room, then tell them! If you don't want your mom calling you for daily check-ins, your grandpa preaching to keep the faith because God has

THE ELEPHANT IN THE ROOM

Ever feel like people are avoiding you because your person died? Like, you go to a party and the crowd seems to dissipate into another room?

Or how about at school pick-up, when another mom is walking your way, sends a quick nod and wave, then bee-lines it out of there to avoid talking about it.

Or, at a coffee date with a girlfriend catching up about life and she won't ask you *"how you are feeling?"* or even acknowledge the fact your person just died (when you know she's read about it all over social media and definitely talked to all of your friends)?

If you feel people are avoiding you like the plague, it's because they are. This hurts. I see you.

a plan, or another freaking casserole dropped on your doorstep, then by all means say something!

This also means silencing any critics of your grief. The way you grieve is your business! You don't owe anything to anyone. So if someone making you feel like you should be doing anything other than what you are doing, this is your permission slip to communicate why criticism is not helpful or . . . to LET IT GO!

Normalize How Hard This Is For Everyone

Before voicing your needs or communicating a boundary (which I'll get to in a sec), it's always helpful to normalize how hard navigating a loss is for everyone. Explain that we live in a grief-averse society that doesn't know how to deal with pain and loss. This neutralizes the situation by showing that you have compassion for where your friend or family member is coming from too.

Become a Grief Educator

If you have picked up this book it tells me that you are curious—that you are seeking advice, education, and knowledge around grief. So this is your opportunity to USE IT! Put it into action. Start educating your friends and family about what grievers—YOU—actually need. How platitudes and advice aren't always helpful and that just sitting with you in your pain or simply listening can feel so supportive. Again—** if you are ready and able to**— remind them that it's not their fault that they didn't know, and acknowledge that they were just trying to help.

Set Boundaries

Even though you've put on your grief educator hat and are advocating for your needs, some friends and family just do not listen! Maybe it's your father-in-law who is also grieving the loss of his son while you are grieving your husband, and your grief looks totally different. You might want to talk openly about your husband to keep his spirit alive, but his approach is to stuff it down and suck it up because he's from a generation that doesn't welcome emotions—and surely he knows best!

If your best efforts fall upon deaf ears, it's okay to set a boundary! This could be:

- Communicating to grandpa that at your house, your husband will be talked about.
- That if he can't respect your wishes, then it's okay if he doesn't come over.
- And if he tells *your* son that *boys don't cry* he will be asked to leave.

Boundaries redefine a relationship and help everyone feel safe. I want to remind you that a boundary doesn't have to be permanent! It can just be temporary—or even held only during acute grief when emotions are high and everyone is running a bit raw.

Choose You

Not everyone will be able to meet your needs, honor your boundaries, or believe that you are your best guide. And as hard as this is to reconcile, you unfortunately can't force anyone to understand or change. All that you can do is focus on your response—your behavior and actions moving forward. This is called *staying in your lane* and it will save you a lot of time and precious energy when dealing with friends and family who don't understand.

When I say choose you, I mean honor what you need and desire at all costs— even if it means pausing a friendship or letting go of a relationship entirely. I know this is so hard to do and brings up more grief, but think about it this

I 1000000 PERCENT GET HOW HARD THIS IS!

In the first year of grief, I received a lot of criticism from certain family members regarding how much I offloaded my kids to babysitters so that I could write about my story of loss on my blog and workout to move through my emotions. To the critics, this looked irresponsible and selfish—*My kids had already lost their father, they needed their mom! Why was Mom off wasting time writing her blog and constantly exercising?*

What they didn't understand was that I needed that space to survive! I was a better mom when I made space for myself to process my emotions and feel them—even if the modality seemed silly to others.

I had to communicate my needs to my family members and explain why the blog and exercise were so important to my healing. Then I set a boundary. I said . . .

If you cannot surround me with unconditional love and support, then I don't have space for you in my life right now.

These words seemed harsh but they changed everything—for me and my relationships. I was the expert—the grief guide—and others learned to trust that I knew what was best for me.

Okay, so now that we've covered the sources of unnecessary suffering, I invite you to review these past couple of pages and reflect on the following journal prompts.

way . . . you are letting go of people who are adding to your suffering to make space for others who support your, get you, empower you, and will elevate you to the new version of you post-loss.

Journal Prompts to Reduce Your Suffering

In this section I covered three sources of potential unnecessary suffering that are likely making your grief even worse. Remember, pain is part of the process . . . suffering is optional. If you can reduce the suffering around your experience of grieving, then all that's left is to feel it.

Source 1: Stories

- How is CONDITIONING shaping my experience of loss and my perception of how I should grieve? Consider your religious beliefs, culture, popular culture, and entertainment.

- Do I have an OLD WOUND that is potentially amplifying my grief in the present? Consider your childhood, parental figures, and past losses or trauma.

- How is my FAMILY UPBRINGING impacting the way I grieve? Consider how emotions, death, and struggle were handled and perceived.

Source 2: Guilt

- Do I have feelings of guilt around my person's death? If so, what are they?

- What do I wish I did differently? Am I still holding regrets?

- Am I searching for someone to blame for my person's death? Would I rather feel guilty than powerless?

- Can I hold compassion for these guilty thoughts, as I try my best to challenge and release them?

Source 3: Friends and Family

- What do I need right now?

- What do I **not** need?

- Am I communicating this? Why, or why not?

- How can I use my knowledge of grief to help others better support me?

- Is there a boundary I need to set? If so, what would it look like?

- If someone cannot honor my boundary, am I willing to put the relationship on pause?

Asking yourself these questions will help you bring awareness—or **consciousness**—to your thoughts so that you can notice which ones are serving you and, more importantly, which ones are not. Once you become aware of these additional sources of suffering, you can begin to separate them from the pure grief and allow yourself to just feel it.

Because **grief is love.**

To get to it . . . you've got to move through pain.

Grief, I've learned, is really just love. It's all the love you want to give, but cannot. All that unspent love gathers up in the corners of your eyes, the lump in your throat, and in that hollow part of your chest. Grief is just love with no place to go. —Jamie Anderson

---

Move through It! (How to Cope)

Okay, we just covered why it's so hard to feel your emotions and how this actually creates more suffering in grief. You reduce resistance and preserve precious energy when you learn to *flow* with your emotions instead of *fight* them, so that you can embrace grief as the unexpressed love for your person.

This work is key to integrating your loss and carrying your person with you as you move forward—because by loving them, and losing them . . . you are who you are now!

Grief doesn't have to #SUCK.

I remember scrolling the social media feeds of other widows' accounts and I kept seeing the hashtag #griefsucks. I thought to myself, *if I'm going to feel this grief for life, then I'd rather not want it to suck.* I asked myself how could I change my relationship to my grief? How could I accept it? Embrace it . . . maybe even love it?

I noticed how subtle shifts like getting curious about my emotions instead of criticizing myself for having them reduced any anxiety or tension around the way I was feeling. If I could simply name that I was sad or angry, approve of the emotion, then just feel it . . . I felt better a lot faster than if I shamed myself for feeling a certain way.

TURN YOUR CRITICISM INTO CURIOSITY

When you are feeling an emotion in grief, stop, then bring awareness to your thoughts. What is the first thing you say? Maybe it's . . .

What's wrong with me?

I shouldn't be feeling this way.

I thought I should be better by now.

Instead of criticizing yourself for the feeling, try to get curious about it. Shift *what's wrong with me?* to *why am I feeling this way?*

If you think you shouldn't be feeling a certain way, ask yourself why not. (You probably have a very valid reason.)

Notice if you are qualifying your emotions (good or bad, right or wrong) or using them as a mark of progress in your grief (for example, if you are feeling sadness you are worse, if you are happy you are better).

Control your thoughts or energy around the emotion so that you can approve it, validate it, and just feel it!

Grief is a natural and normal response to a loss. Due to the intensity and range of feelings and emotions that arise in the grieving process, the experience can feel overwhelming and confusing. However, these responses are REAL because you are feeling them. Your feelings and emotions exist for a reason!

It's the thoughts, beliefs, and stories that we make up about our emotions that add to your suffering.

"There is no such thing as a bad emotion."

"Feelings are feelings. They all deserve reverence."

The Change Triangle

I learned about the Change Triangle when I read Hilary Jacobs Hendel's book *It's Not Always Depression* during my binge of self-help books and widow memoirs to help me navigate what I was experiencing after my husband's death. Like I said, getting **curious** about this stuff validates a lot of what you're experiencing.

The Change Triangle is a tool to help you get reacquainted with your core emotions and to connect with your true self. The concept of the Change Triangle was first described by Dr. David Malan in the 1970s and later by Diana Fosha in her book *The Transforming Power of Affect.*

This model shows how we often block our core emotions (many that arise in grief) with defenses (anything we do to avoid the feeling) and with inhibitory emotions (having emotions about your emotions).

In order to get to your core emotions, you have to bring down your **defenses—** numbing out on social media, busying yourself with work, dulling sensations with drugs or alcohol, or anything else that pulls you away from feeling a feeling. You also have to release your **inhibitory emotions—**your shame at feeling angry, anxiety when you experience a wave of deep sadness, or guilt for feeling happy again!

Then you get to your **core emotions.** These emotions inform us about our environment. They are hard-wired in the middle parts of our brain—meaning they are NOT subject to conscious control. Hendel explains . . .

Triggered by the environment (like someone important to us dying and all the material changes that we encounter in life without them), *each core emotion is pre-wired to set off a host of physiological reactions that prime us for an action that is meant to be adaptive, like running from danger.*

Your core emotions are a response. You've got to feel them! And once you do—once you release these emotions—you get to your **openhearted state of authentic self.** This is where you feel calm and connected to yourself; where you can get curious about what was coming up for you and hold compassion for your pain; where you can access the clarity about your next step forward; and access the courage to take that step.

THE TANTRUM

When I teach the Change Triangle to my clients, I tell them to imagine a toddler having a temper tantrum. If you have kids, you know that you cannot argue, talk, or even relate to a toddler when they are in the middle of a tantrum. They are incapable of reasoning or hearing you at all because their whole nervous system is in a state of fight or flight. You have to wait for them to move the energy through—to calm down. To get to their openhearted state of authentic self when they are ready for a solution.

The same is true for YOU!

When you are in the middle of feeling a big emotion, it's hard to think clearly or look for a solution. So if you feel a wave of sadness, an outburst of anger, or are overwhelmed, try to simply name the emotion, own it, feel it, and release it. (See the moveTHRU Method on page 74.)

Emotions are energy in motion, so once you release this energy you will generally feel calmer and more connected. Think of how you feel after a good cry. Maybe you feel drained and tired—like you've realized something—but you are also calm and centered. This is the state we want to live in for most of our lives, when we are emotionally regulated and calm so that we can respond or act with intention, look for solutions, and begin to adapt to life without our person.

Coping Strategies

Coping strategies give you tools to regulate your nervous system and move through your emotions in a way that feels safe and supportive—because I get it, it's hard to feel the deep pain of loss! Some of the emotions in grief can get really big and overwhelming, and while we do need to feel pain in order to heal it, there is such a thing as *too much, too soon, too quickly!* So finding supportive ways to cope with your emotions helps to soften the experience of feeling them.

There's a plethora of outlets for coping with grief. I like to choose mine based on what feeling or emotion I'm experiencing at a given time. For instance, if I'm struggling to work through a guilty thought, I'll write it down and journal about why I feel guilty, what moral code I believe I'm actually breaking, and try to challenge it through written word. Writing is helpful for breaking down complex thoughts, while movement might be more supportive for a more embodied emotion like anger. For example, whenever I felt the building fury and resentment over my solo parenting situation, I would move through these emotions by attending a kickboxing class or doing a strenuous HIIT workout.

There is no such thing as a right or wrong way to cope with grief, and what works for me or another griever might be totally different from what feels supportive for you. Start by asking yourself the following questions:

- How am I feeling?
- What do I need?
- How do I get it?

If you can name the feeling or emotion, it's easier to understand what you need to in order to cope with it. For example, if it's an **embodied emotion** like anger, sadness, or anxiety, finding a way to physically move through the emotion to feel it might be supportive. If it's a **feeling**—meaning it's driven by a thought—processing the emotion with a therapist or coach, or by journaling about it, might do the trick.

Even if you can't name the exact feeling or emotion, I invite you to close your eyes (if you feel safe), take a deep breath and just ask yourself **what would feel most supportive or nourishing for me right now?** It's so easy to get caught up in the ways you think you "should" be grieving. This practice helps you get out of your head and into your body so that you can hear your intuition speaking loud and clear. Let it guide you down your path toward healing.

If you are looking for inspiration on ways to cope, here are some other ideas that you can pull from!

FEELINGS VS. EMOTIONS

Feelings: These are expressed consciously, meaning they are often driven or accompanied by a thought (which might be influenced by cultural, religious, societal, and family upbringing). This is where consciousness comes into play; once you change your *thought*, you can change your *feeling!*

Emotions: These are "energy in motion" and are associated with the bodily reactions that are activated. They are hard-wired in our brain and experienced both subconsciously and consciously. They manifest in the unconscious mind.

The key difference is that **feelings are conscious and are driven by a thought, whereas emotions, while also subconscious or unconscious, sometimes need to be brought to the surface to be untangled, felt, and understood.** Because emotions trigger a physiological response, movement can be a wonderful modality to feel and relate to them.

Toolkit of Coping Strategies for Grief

Talking about it: Whether it's with a friend, family member, therapist, coach, or grief group, talking about your loss will help you to process your loss and your complex feelings or thoughts associated with it. As you process out loud, emotions typically arise, helping you to *feel* it too!

Journaling: Writing and reflecting on how you are feeling what you are struggling with, and how much you miss your person, helps you to dive into the pain and process complex thoughts. Writing letters to your person can also be very therapeutic and cathartic.

Exercise: (My favorite!) Going for a hard workout, swim, run, walk, or dance class. (I'll get into why this is so effective in the next section.)

Somatic therapy: Exercise actually falls under the larger umbrella of somatic therapies, which connect the mind to the body in healing modalities. Because grief and trauma are also stored in the body, somatic therapies are extremely effective.

Exploring nervous system regulation techniques: If your feelings feel really big and overwhelming—like you are on the verge of a panic attack—exploring breath-work, visualization and grounding exercises or EFT tapping with a licensed provider would be supportive strategies for you. Some of these might also fall under the category of somatic practices.

Connecting with nature: This one is so simple! There's something incredibly healing about being in nature; maybe it's the sense of grounding you feel when your feet touch the earth, or that you are connected to something greater when you are in the presence of a vast mountainside or open sea.

Practicing self-care: Again, so simple, yet something that we often forget to do! Basic practices like getting enough sleep, drinking water, eating nourishing foods, making space to be alone with your feelings, and not over programming yourself right now will help you to cope.

Sharing your story on social media: Seriously, I did this and it's a great way to process your emotions, have your grief witnessed by others who comment on your posts, and even to find meaning.

Exploring the *WOO*: Sound baths, energy healings, aromatherapy, acupuncture, and ecstatic dancing, among other less-traditional healing modalities, can be an effective way to cope because they appeal to all the senses (or realms), opening up different pathways to healing. Even if you are skeptical, I invite you to keep an open mind and explore it all.

You never know what modality might really shift things for you!

Beyond Talking about It

As soon as my husband passed away, friends and family insisted that I start talking to a therapist. So every week I spent an hour processing my thoughts and feelings with a licensed professional who clearly had studied and written dissertations on grief, but had never actually **lived it.**

Not only did I feel isolated talking about my loss in a confined office space, but I would leave each session still feeling heavy. The conversation helped me process everything that was happening in my upside-down world at that moment, but it was as if these thoughts were disconnected from my body. I craved a way to simply FEEL—without words and in a more embodied way.

Why Movement Helps You Move through Grief

Most of us know that exercise releases endorphins—and endorphins make you happy! So if you are in deep grief, it makes sense that moving your body would make you feel better. But there's more actual science as to why movement is such an effective coping mechanism for grief. Here's why:

Grief is not just stored in your brain! It's also stored in your body. The problem with traditional grief therapy (talking about it) is that emotional memory and trauma is stored within your body. Research suggests that organs, tissues, skin, muscle, and endocrine glands all have peptide receptors on them that can access and store emotional information. This means that emotional memory is stored in many places in the body, not just, or even primarily, in the brain.

So verbalizing your emotions in traditional grief therapy only makes up one half of the equation—you have to find a way to FEEL them too. Talking about it can absolutely bring up emotions to be felt, but there is typically additional unprocessed grief that's in your body too.

Break the cycle of negative thought. Think of all the changes you are trying to navigate since your loved one passed way. Although you're cognitively aware of all these changes, your body responds to them as a threat because it's all foreign and new. These perceived threats create a stress response (physical, emotional, or psychological strain) and sends your nervous system into a state of hyperactivity—your flight-or-fight survival response gets caught in a loop.

When this happens, you might feel frozen. Feelings of anxiety, overwhelm, sadness, or guilt become all-encompassing. And as all of your attention gets fixed on these negative thought patterns, it feels impossible to break the cycle, and so thus you start to feel "stuck."

A NOTE ON THERAPY

Therapy is a wonderful way to unpack subconscious beliefs, past trauma, and wounds from your childhood that might affect your current experience of grief (and life). But what many grievers and myself have found is that therapy wasn't super useful in the early stages of their loss.

I love therapy, and I still see my therapist weekly to this day, but in early grief I stopped going altogether because what I needed was a proactive plan to quite literally survive. What I really needed early on was:

- Tools and insights to navigate my current situation (not to unpack the past).

- Strategies to regulate my emotions.

- A community of other grievers to make me feel less alone.

If you do choose to pursue a therapist, make sure that they are grief-informed or have personally experienced a loss. Sadly, the aversion to grief even permeates the world of mental health, where many professionals actually view it a symptom to be cured as opposed to a universal human experience. That's when I discovered the power of movement to move through grief.

Exercise was how I experienced my emotions and felt my feelings during the early stages of loss. While I felt trapped in my mind, I experienced a sense of freedom with every burpee, a hint of courage with every rep of a heavy weight, and a glimmer of hope with every drop of sweat fleeing my body.

When I felt a certain emotion, I would choose a workout to experience and then release it. For anger I would attend a kickboxing class, for anxiety I would jump on a spin bike or go for a run, for sadness I would walk in nature or attend a gentle yoga flow. It was as if the physical pain and challenge of my workout mirrored the emotional pain and struggle that I was experiencing.

Moving through my emotions helped me to feel them in a way that talking about them could not. And, most importantly, exercise made me strong in my new normal that was making me feel powerless.

Have *you* felt this way in grief?

Stuck is a feeling of overwhelm and a sense of paralysis or powerlessness that might arise after your loved one dies. It's that feeling of wanting to move forward with life, but you just can't because everything feels impossible (your attention gets fixed on the negative thought pattern).

So what do you do when your mind is convincing you that you are incapable of moving forward?

You prove it wrong by moving your body!

Movement breaks the cycle of negative thought. And if you want to dive deep into this topic about how grief and trauma are stored in the body, there's a plethora of research and studies by Peter Levine, PhD (the father of somatic therapies) and even an amazing book by Bessel van Der Kolk, MD, called *The Body Keeps the Score*.

Movement provides you with temporary relief from the pain. Ever heard the term "in the zone?" What this common phrase alludes to is the concept of **flow**, which was named by psychologist Mihaly Csikszentmihalyi in 1975. In positive psychology, a flow state is defined as:

The mental state in which a person performing some activity is fully immersed in a feeling of energized focus and full involvement, resulting in enjoyment.

Think about a time when you were fully engrossed in an activity. Maybe it was a deep conversation with a friend, planting flowers in your garden, cooking a new recipe or completing a challenging run? As you focus on the task at hand, time seemingly flies by and the simple act of being in process brings you energy . . . and even joy!

Exercises like yoga, running, biking, dancing, or your favorite group fitness class are an easy way to get into flow state, because you're forced to focus on the present physical demand. Not all flow states need to be physical, so I invite you to explore an activity that feels supportive for you.

Regardless of which activity you choose, finding ways to be in flow while grieving can provide you with temporary relief from the pain, which can feel like a lifeline on days when the emotions hit hard.

Toolkit to Move through Common Emotions in Grief

Emotions are energy in motion. Some have a high, intense energy, while others feel heavy or more subtle. Because of the different energies, various types of movement will help you to embody them in order to move through them. Here are some exercises you can try for each one:

Sadness

- Walk in nature
- Gentle stretching
- Restorative yoga
- Breath work exercises
- Meditation
- Tai chi

Anger

- Scream into a pillow
- Pound or throw a pillow
- Slam a shoe or a ball on the floor
- Sit on the floor and pound the ground, or clench your fists and pound your thighs
- Visit a rage room and break things!
- Go kickboxing or do a HIIT workout
- Lift heavy weights

Shock

- Walk in nature
- Grounding exercises
- Yoga
- Barre (low impact, but you feel the physical burn)
- Swimming
- Slower exercises that demand more presence

Anxiety

- Running
- Biking
- Anything cardio-related
- Grounding exercises
- Power or vinyasa yoga

Loneliness

- Partner sports
- Team sports
- Group fitness class (reminds you of community)
- Yoga (brings awareness to your thoughts)
- Meditation

The move*THRU* Method

Although I discovered the power of movement to help me cope with grief *intuitively*, after researching the subject and finding evidence to back my findings, I created the move*THRU* Method to help other grievers take advantage of this highly effective healing modality.

The move*THRU* Method is my eight-step sequence to help you name, approve of, and feel your emotions to get to a clear, connected state of being where you can make the necessary mindset shifts to move forward.

The sequence follows the acronym move*THRU*, and it goes as follows:

Motivation

The first step in the move*THRU* method is get to curious about your emotions (instead of criticizing yourself for having them) by seeking to understand the reason behind them—the motivation. This is an invitation to simply notice how you are feeling, bring awareness to that sensation, and exploring why you are feeling a certain way.

Ownership

Next, I invite you to own the emotion. Accept it and approve it! All too often grievers try to suppress what they are feeling or just pretend the emotions don't exist out of fear that they "shouldn't" be feeling a certain way. But you can't feel the emotion without acknowledging that it exists. Name your emotions without judgment, shame, or beating yourself up about it. Your feelings are valid!

Validation

If you are experiencing a feeling, that means it's real—thus it's valid! Whether it's actually true (meaning it might be driven by a limiting belief or old story), it's there for a reason and so it demands to be felt. Remind yourself that your feelings are valid and it's okay to feel this way.

Experience

Experiencing your emotions means finding a way to **feel them.** You can embody them through movement, write about them, talk about them—or refer back to my coping strategies section for more ideas! I'm a firm believer that different emotions require unique healing modalities, so tune in and ask yourself—*what do I need right now?*

Through

After you feel the emotions, you literally move them through your body. This stage refers to the release—this is the calm after the storm, after the big cry or burst of anger where you feel calmer and more connected. The state where resilience is born and you can make the necessary mindset shifts to move forward.

Honor and Reframe

I group these two steps together because they address the duality needed to hold both the tragedy of your experience and the new, reframed perspective that is required to integrate your loss. (I'll touch on duality much more in Part Three). Reframing your experience of loss helps you to see it through a different lens; it allows you to search for new angles beyond the pain and suffering—like noticing your increased resilience and inner strength and newfound appreciation for life—which gives it new meaning. These two steps invite you to honor everything that you are going through—the pain, the sadness, and the devastation—and encourages you to seek a new perspective. Can you hold . . .

The grief and the gratitude.

The pain and the love.

The death and the rebirth.

These concepts are all related. Without one, there is not the others.

I have learned there is no joy without hardship.
There is no pleasure without pain. Would we know the comfort of peace
without the distress of war —Elisabeth Kübler-Ross

Understanding

The final stage of the move*THRU* Method is understanding. After you've owned the feeling, trusted in its validity, and felt it to move the energy through, this is where you get curious again, seeking key takeaways and lessons from the wisdom of your body. Was the anxiety about taking on too much right now? Or was it about unprocessed grief? Was the outburst of anger truly about my kids making a mess? Or was it because I had to clean it up alone without their father?

Your feelings and emotions exist for a reason. While most of the world tries to numb out and silence these emotions because they are incredibly uncomfortable, your work is lean into them and feel them in order to uncover their underlying cause. Ask yourself, what is this emotion telling me? What is it trying to say?

This practice of listening to your emotions won't just guide you through grief, it will also be a crucial compass for re-discovering who you are and rebuilding your life.

Grief is absolutely the price you pay for love! As grievers, your healing work and journey forward into life without your person is about learning how to remember with more love than pain.

This process of integration requires feeling your grief and moving through the pain. In the beginning this feels impossible because your grief is so unfamiliar. So I invite you to think of grief as a muscle that with practice and exercise becomes stronger with time. The sensations become familiar and you learn how to ride the waves. You will be able to understand which milestones (death anniversaries, holidays, birthdays) tend to trigger you so you are more prepared ahead of time, and you feel more empowered when it comes to navigating them if you have techniques to help you cope and ground down.

So as you move through grief and feel the pain, remember:

- The pain is part of the process and you are moving through the pain to access the love.
- Your emotions are not good or bad or right or wrong, they are all valid and deserve reverence.

Part Three

Grow

※

You had no choice in this.
Your person died
without your consent.
You took back control over
your life by choosing to adapt.
And in doing so,
you were forced to expand.

After Ian's death, I felt his absence in every way. From the second I woke up in my big, empty bed, to going back to sleep at night alone again, there was a noticeable void everywhere I turned.

The void met me as the sun rose, while sipping coffee with no one to talk to; then it followed me as I dropped my kids off at school and drove home without a passenger.

The void met me when the washing machine broke and I had a tough financial decision to make. It met me on major holidays like Father's Day or when one of our children's birthdays approached. It met me at the airport while taming two wild kids and slugging luggage around; and at my kids' baseball games or kindergarten graduations as I saw other "full" families together.

The void met me at functions with friends, where I quickly became the fifth wheel; or at restaurants when my dad would blurt out my tragic story to any stranger who would listen.

It met me with every breath that I took while living life without him.

What made the void hurt even more was the lack of awareness from friends and family. These losses were invisible to them, but to me—they were material! I felt guilty for grieving the role of the father figure probably more than Ian himself in the first year after his death. But the absence of my life partner and father of my children rocked our family's foundation to the core. I had to grieve all the subtle ways in which Ian was interwoven into this dynamic in order to build a new one.

As I moved through the grief that arose from each invisible loss, I was also forced to fill the void left in its place. I had to adapt! Someone had to fix the broken washing machine, make important decisions, and raise the kids—even if it meant doing it alone. As I became my own handyman and also learned to rely on others for help; as I dug deep to control my anger and not unleash it on my kids; as I connected to my intuition to make important decisions on my own—I was forced to stretch! And in doing so I **grew.**

Noticing my growth shined light in the darkness of the void. Where there once was grief, there was now a sense of **gratitude.**

Where there once was pain, there was now a sense of **pride.**

Where there once was resentment, there was now a sense of **resilience.**

It wasn't like the grief, pain, and resentment were gone, but other emotions were there too. I started paying attention to how my loss was changing me and was actually making me a stronger, more compassionate, and grateful human being.

If fact, I remember the distinct moment on an airplane thinking how just two years ago the exact flight would have triggered me into a bout of resentment and self-pity—having to see other complete families vacationing together. But now, the trip was easier. I had adapted. I couldn't believe how far we had come! I knew exactly how to entertain my kids, how to ask for help, and how to regulate my emotions if the inevitable meltdown was to arise. I felt an overwhelming sense of pride. We—the THREE of us—were doing it. We were okay!

At times I felt guilty for feeling this way. If I felt good or, do I dare say excited, about the growth I was experiencing, my mind quickly made me feel like that was wrong. I thought that if I wasn't feeling pain, then I must be abandoning Ian. How could I feel okay after the love of my life and father of my children had died? It didn't make sense. I thought that I would hurt forever and that the pain was my lifeline back to him.

But in getting curious about grief, I learned that grief is love. And it wasn't the pain that connected me to Ian . . . it was the love!

My grief was evolving and I was remembering with more love than pain. And the growth that I was experiencing was starting to give my loss new meaning.

I was proud of my family of three—and of my inner resilience and strength.

I took less for granted; the small things simply didn't matter to me anymore—I was alive! I was open to new possibilities in life, I had already walked myself through fire so I could literally do anything now.

And when my mind tried to convince me that it was not okay to look toward the future that I was rebuilding with excitement, I leaned on the concept of duality. My gratitude for life didn't diminish my grief, nor did my pride minimize my pain. I learned that you could actually hold two conflicting emotions all at once and both could be true at the very same time. The mere concept of duality and learning how to embrace it expanded me even more.

The experience of loss had rocked me to my core. In the rupture of it all I was forced to stretch, expand and grow. And I was excited the version of myself who I was becoming!

Who would she be?

What would she create?

Now that she had walked herself through fire . . . she was fireproof!

Why You Grow through Grief

To my surprise, the growth that I experienced after my husband's death was not unique. In reading Facebook COO Sheryl Sandberg's book, *Option B*, I learned about resilience and how navigating life-altering loss or surviving any type of adversity can result in growth.

The growth that I witnessed in myself was not uncommon. In fact, there was a whole term for it backed by decades of research: **post-traumatic grief.**

Grief is a cocoon from which we emerge new. —Glennon Doyle

Post-Traumatic Growth

In the 1990s, Richard Tedeschi, PhD, and Lawrence Calhoun, PhD, coined the term Post-Traumatic Growth (PTG) after studying survivors of trauma. The results suggested a positive psychological change experienced as a result of struggling with highly challenging, highly stressful life circumstances. The concept of PTG is widely accepted in psychology and is still being explored and studied today.

In terms of grief and loss, PTG includes the **positive changes that might take place in the aftermath of someone dying (i.e., the trauma).** Because trauma is subjective to each individual, for PTG to occur the event must be seismic enough to shake your belief in a just world, robbing you of the sense that life is controllable, predictable, and meaningful.

Traumatic events like the death of a loved one make it hard to see new possibilities. These experiences rip away your present and tear apart your hopes for the future. They rock you to the core—where you are forced to stretch, find your edge, and **seek a new belief system about the world in which we exist.**

This is where growth and transformation begin!

Although it can be extremely difficult to grasp, the disappearance of one possible self can free us to imagine a new possible self. —Sheryl Sandberg, *Option B*

Types of Post-Traumatic Growth

According to Richard Tedeschi, PhD, and Lawrence Calhoun, PhD, in the *Journal of Traumatic Stress,* 1996, there are five areas of post-traumatic growth. As you read through each type, I invite you to consider if you have experienced growth in this area and reflect on how you have grown from your loss.

1. **Appreciation for Life**

    Trauma brings you face to face with your mortality. You realize the fragility of life and that your time here is finite. With this awareness, you might take less for granted or find more gratitude in each small moment, knowing that the future is uncertain or not guaranteed.

    How does this apply in your experience?

2. **Relationships with Others**

    Traumatic experiences force you to evaluate where you feel connected, seen, and supported! You might let go of relationships that no longer serve you, and in their place create new ones by joining communities that understand your circumstances or align with your growth. You also might experience more compassion for others.

    How have your relationships changed since your person's passing?

3. **New Possibilities in Life**

   Traumatic events like the death of a loved one rock you to your core. Your entire perspective tends to shift. The things that used to be meaningful might not be anymore. You tend to sweat the small things less as you reprioritize your values. You might find yourself shifting your time and energy to align with what matters to you now.

   How has your new perspective on life shifted your priorities?

4. **Personal Strength (Resilience!)**

   Your inner capacity to withstand hardship often increases after a loss. In the face of trauma, you are forced to explore what helps you feel strong and you learn how to access the resources within yourself. This journey includes learning to cope, figuring out how to adapt to life without your loved one, and connecting back to yourself to discover who you are now and what you desire out of life.

   How did your experience of loss make you more resilient?

5. **Spiritual Change**

   Those who have experienced profound loss often feel a shift in spirituality. The loss of a loved one often brings up questions of mortality, afterlife, and spiritual meaning. You might ask yourself—*Why me? Is there a higher purpose? What happens to my person once he or she is gone? Is there a divine plan in order?* These questions are deeply personal and can be processed slowly with time, along the never-ending arch of grief.

   How have my spiritual beliefs shifted since my person's death?

Have you noticed any of these changes within you? If so, how? Write them down and reflect on how your loss has changed you . . . for the better! This is one way to begin searching for new angles beyond the pain and suffering—the foundations of meaning making and changing your narrative on loss. So pay attention to these subtle shifts! (We will address this more in Part Four.)

When you begin to notice your growth and see glimmers of "good" in the "bad," there's a chance you might also feel guilty about it. Your mind can't reconcile how anything positive can come from your loss and positions your growth as some sort of trade-off. You might find yourself thinking, why did my person have to die for me to become more grateful or resilient? Trust me, it happens to all of us!

What's key here is to **remember that you didn't have a choice!** Your person died without your consent. The only choice you had was to move through it—and in the process you grew a ton.

As you begin to witness the positive changes taking place, you also might start to feel better. Immediately your brain creates a story that if you aren't feeling pain, sadness, and deep grief, then you must not love your person anymore. While this feeling is valid (and oh so common), it couldn't be further from the truth.

Grief *is* love! And you aren't connected to your person through the pain. You are connected to them by love.

WHEN YOU FEEL GUILTY FOR YOUR GROWTH

Here are some reminders to refer back to when your mind makes you feel guilty about your growth.

- Your growth does not minimize the tragedy of your loss.

- You don't have to choose between grief and growth or any conflicting emotions—you can hold them all with duality (see page 104).

- You are not connected to your deceased loved one by the pain—you are connected to them by the love.

- Your growth is a product of moving through something really hard. You didn't want your loved one to die, but you chose to adapt. And in doing so, you were forced to expand.

This is just a sign of you doing the work to heal. You've been excavating through all the layers of pain as you moved through your grief, and you have reached the love! Well done, friend.

Growth Happens in the Void

I invite you to imagine yourself walking on a long dirt road. You look behind you and see the life you knew and loved. This life feels like it's within hand's reach but it's also so far away. In fact, the more you move forward, it's like you're creating even more distance. You long for that life. It feels safe and comfortable—it reminds you of home. Every time you look behind you, the pain and sadness rises. You grieve the life that was.

You turn toward the other direction.

In front of you is your new life. It's new, it's scary, and totally foreign—basically a blank slate. The vastness of this terrain makes it feel almost impossible to know how to even start. How do you rebuild an *entire* life? There are no answers, only questions; and the uncertainty of it all feels almost paralyzing. You fear the life that will be.

Try to really see yourself **here.**

Between the life that **was** and what will **be.**

You are right in the middle—the life that **is.**

This is the void.

This is **acceptance!**

And as disorienting, confusing, and uncomfortable as being right in the middle of the void can be, this is the breeding ground for growth and transformation.

Because growth happens when you are forced to change. When you grieve what was, accept what is, and step into what will be.

Here you are in the middle of two distinct lives, but unlike most junctures, you don't have to choose a path. You can carry parts of your past *with* you, into your future through the process of **integration** (like we talked about in Part Two). In fact, the more you allow yourself to feel your grief, maintain a connection to your deceased, and allow their physical absence to guide as you move forward, the more you will grow! The more you will create meaning, alchemize your pain into purpose, and thrive.

The Dual Process Model of Coping with Bereavement

I love Stroebe and Schut's Dual Process Model for Coping with Bereavement as another visual of what I'm describing.

In their model, they separate the process of bereavement into two categories: Loss-Oriented and Restoration-Oriented.

Under the Loss-Oriented category, they include grief-related activities, such as intrusion of big emotions, breaking bonds and emotional ties, denial, and avoidance. While on the Restoration-Oriented side, they share activities related to moving forward, such as attending to life changes, doing new things, and exploring new roles and identities.

Then they place a zigzag line that bounces between the two categories to show how grievers often oscillate between the Loss-Oriented and Restoration-Oriented views, as they navigate everyday life after loss.

You're having to bounce back and forth from the **loss-oriented side** of being consumed by your emotions and trying to grieve everything in your past, to the **restoration-oriented side,** where you're adapting to life and making proactive shifts to move forward. No wonder they call healing **work!**

As much as you are grieving, you are simultaneously **growing.** Because in the void of what *was* you are also being forced to adapt to what *is* (and laying the groundwork for what will *be*). Adaptation takes a degree of stretching; it forces you to your edge—the edge of "normal" and beyond the comfort of what you believed yourself capable. This is uncharted territory and you're being invited to go there.

Some of us mistake the discomfort of growth as a sign that they are regressing or they are doing grief wrong—but **it's the discomfort that creates the change.** Remember, pain is part of the process. They are called growing *pains* for a reason.

Think about it in terms of a physical challenge . . .

When I decided to run my first marathon, I didn't know that I was capable of running a full 26.2 miles. I was playing in the realm of the unknown. So I trained, slowing increasing my milage to gradually adapt to this new goal I had set for myself. The long hours of training were physically painful and mentally challenging, because I was forcing myself to stretch beyond my known capacity. On the day of the race, miles twenty to twenty-six hurt like hell! But I accepted the pain as a part of the process and crossed the finish line.

Discomfort is temporary.

Growth is permanent.

Growth occurs when you get outside of your comfort zone. And there's nothing like a life-altering loss to propel you into the realm of discomfort.

Secondary Losses

As you can see in the Dual Process Model, grief and growth happen hand in hand. So let's focus on the grief side of the model for a second.

You are probably keenly aware by now that you don't just grieve your person. You also grieve those sneaky, secondary losses such as identity, shared decision making, and financial security, just to name a few.

Secondary losses are **invisible, unanticipated losses that only become understood and felt once you are living through them.** They can be just as painful, difficult to accept, and adjust to as the primary loss of your person. Thus, they deserve reverence and space to be grieved.

Think about all the ways your person was integrated into your life. Whatever they touched, whatever they influenced, and whomever they connected with is now

> ## WHEN OTHERS DON'T GET IT
>
> Remember that some friends and family won't likely understand the loss of purpose or the death of your shared dreams and the future that you are also grieving. They can't see it, they've never experienced it, so it's difficult for them to comprehend.
>
> This is where you really have to trust yourself! You don't need anyone's validation to prove these losses worthy of your grief. My best advice is to let go of the need for others to always understand you, and just allow yourself to grieve. Sourcing permission and validation from within is another sign of growth.

changed by their physical absence. A loved one's death creates a ripple effect of losses that are invisible to the outside world but feel tumultuous to the griever.

This list is certainly not complete, but I invite you to **take account of the secondary losses that feel most alive for you in your grief.**

Name them.

Write them down.

Allow yourself to grieve them!

Feeling the pain of these losses helps you to **accept** them. And once you accept them, you shift from a **why me?** (victim mindset) to a **what now?** (survivor mindset). You start to seek ways to fill the void and make the necessary changes to move forward. You bounce over to the "restoration side" of the model and grow alongside your grief.

Common Secondary Losses

Here are some common secondary losses that I've seen clients experience, and that I've also seen in my own grief journey.

Loss of Identity

I like to explain the loss of identity using a Venn diagram. In one circle is you. In the other circle is your person. And where the circles converge is your relationship together. Depending on how intermeshed your lives were, the circle in the middle could be really big or small.

When your person died, the *physical* relationship died too! (I stress physical because you can absolutely maintain a relationship with your person in spirit and I highly suggest you explore this as you grieve and move forward. If you missed this, go back to Part One for some ideas!).

So with the physical relationship essentially gone, it can literally feel like a piece of you is missing. Where you were once felt whole, **you now feel like a sliver of who you used to be.** It's as though part of you died with your person . . .

LIFE-DEATH-REBIRTH CYCLE

When I think about the loss of identity, I like to remember that everything in life is connected. The pattern of life, death, and rebirth is highlighted best in nature—in the changing of the seasons—where in fall the trees and plants begin to brown and die, then the snow covers everything in the deadly winter, all for new life to re-emerge in the spring. Endings and beginnings are one and the same. Life, death, and rebirth are part of an endless connected cycle.

Think of a serpent shedding its skin in a continuous renewal of its life cycle. Or the caterpillar that enters the chrysalis and literally becomes a pile of mush before it emerges from the cocoon as a beautiful butterfly. We are continuously grieving old parts of ourselves, allowing old versions, roles, and identities to die in order to continuously grow and evolve.

With my loss, there was a unique version of me that existed when my husband was alive. When he died, a piece of me died too. And in the void, new parts of myself were born.

In loving him and in losing him, I am who I am today.

If this concept lands with you, get outside and see it reflected in nature. Death, endings, and change doesn't have to be scary or bad—it's literally a part of life itself!

And in many ways, it did.

Your identity is **who you are.** In our society, we often define identity solely by the roles we wear—husband, wife, father, mother, teacher, lawyer, doctor, etc. Identity becomes very externalized, defined primarily by ego roles. So when we lose these outer constructs, we don't know who we are anymore.

When I lost my husband I was no longer a wife. My identity shifted to widow.

When my kids lost their father I also grieved their mother. That version of Mom died with Daddy.

This happens with other types of losses, too, not just with death.

When my dad retired he was no longer a doctor. He literally didn't know who he was anymore.

You might find yourself trying to force yourself back into an old version of yourself that you were prior to your person's death. But you no longer fit! That version of you could only exist when your person was alive—your relationship to them defined parts of you. You must grieve that past role and identity in order to accept who you are now—the integrated version of you.

When we grieve these roles, it's as if there is no structure or parameter on how to define ourselves anymore. *Who am I without being wife? Who am I without being a mom? Who am I without my CEO title?* Identity loss can feel painful, bleak, and disorienting. So if you feel this way, please know it's so normal!

The process of getting to know yourself again is slow, healing work that takes time and lots of self-inquiry—which I'll cover more in Part Four: Thrive. For now, remember that your identity is SO much more than the roles you occupied. YOU are more than a job title or a relationship.

You will be whole again but you will never be the same.
Nor should you be the same, nor would you want to. —Elisabeth Kübler-Ross

Ask yourself:

- What are my inherent strengths?
- How would my closest friends and family describe me?
- When I think about myself as a child, what was I like?

Meet yourself at your **essence**. And if you're wanting to dive into identity work now, go ahead and jump to Part Four!

Loss of Purpose

If identity is who you are, then **purpose is what you do.** And because *what you do* informs *who you are,* (especially in our culture) these concepts get confused as meaning the same thing. While they are absolutely related, they are not entirely exclusive.

Purpose is a function of *doing.* It encompasses all of the ways we spend our time and how we decide to make an impact. Your purpose is motived by what matters to you now—which is driven by your core values.

Before your loss, your purpose might have been tied up with your loved one's.

Maybe you were their caregiver during their terminal illness, so most of your time was spent taking them to the doctor, giving them medication, and helping them feel comfortable. Caregiving became your primary purpose.

Maybe you were your person's mother, so most of your time was spent getting them ready for school, tucking them into bed at night, and shuffling them around to soccer practice. Child-rearing became your primary purpose.

Maybe you were your person's best friend, so most of your time was spent hanging out at coffee shops together, playing frisbee in the park, or calling each other at night to hear how your date from Bumble went. Creating meaningful connections was a part of your purpose.

Whatever the relationship was, you spent a lot of time with your person. And in their absence, there's now a lot of empty time and space. **What you did was informed by them,** and now you have to fill this void all by yourself.

The loss of purpose can make life feel pretty meaningless at times. It's like you are walking around aimlessly, disconnected and numb—with no real direction or focus moving forward. It's okay to feel this way.

Again, allow yourself to grieve the loss of purpose—lean into the emptiness of that void. Then, when you are ready, start to get **curious** about your core values and priorities. It's likely that they've changed since your person's death (remember, this is a sign of your growth).

Ask yourself:

- What matters to me now?
- What lights me up and excites me?
- What activity would my person like to do that I can I do now to honor their legacy?

Loss of the Future and Possibility

After a loss, you don't just grieve the past, **you also grieve the future.** Death robs you of possibility—the life that *could have been* with your person.

Think about it.

From the second you laid eyes on your person—whether it was your child, brother, best friend, parent, or lover—you dreamed up a future story *with them in it.* Whether it's thinking that your dad would be there to walk you down the aisle at your wedding, or having your partner to play cribbage with as you grew old together, there is always a future that is lost when your person dies.

This loss of what *could have been* is also connected to the loss of purpose, as well as shared dreams, hopes, and aspirations. Maybe you and your person dreamed of taking an exotic backpacking trip to Colombia together, and now you find yourself without a travel buddy?

Maybe you thought you'd both retire to finally build the non-profit you were passionate about launching, and now your business partner is gone?

These future losses hurt so much and will continue to resurface whenever you reach a new milestone without your person. Another wedding anniversary

COULD HAVE VS. SHOULD HAVE BEEN

When my husband died, I found myself stuck in the repeating thought of *Ian should be here. HE should be teaching Theo how to ride his bike and watching Izzy at her first dance recital.*

A helpful mindset shift was recognizing that the word *should* implied that his time with me and the kids and our future was guaranteed, when in reality nothing is guaranteed! The future was never his, mine, or ours to begin with.

I realized that at any second of any hour of any day, I could walk outside and get hit by a car, or a friend might call with news of a cancer diagnosis. The world was highly unpredictable and chaotic and the only certainty in life was RIGHT NOW.

Once I understood that Ian's death didn't rob us of our entire future—it robbed us of the *possibility* of one—I was able to release my attachment to our future story together. It wasn't mine to being with. And as a result, I found more gratitude for the time we were granted and my presence in the now.

spent without your partner, a birthday with no one in person to celebrate with, and every future holiday dinner with an empty seat at the table.

Again, my invitation to you is to allow yourself to grieve these future losses *first*. Then access the peace and connectedness within yourself to start creating your own dreams again. Take this work slowly. Trying to rebuild an entire future without your person can feel overwhelming . . . so take one step at a time.

In Part Four I'll teach you how to connect back to your purpose and identity to help you envision a future that you're truly excited about. This is where imagination and creativity come into play!

For now, ask yourself:

- How can I honor my person by doing some of the things they were passionate about?
- Can I live out some of their dreams for them?

- How can I live my life right now and create a future that my person would be proud of?

Loss of Confidence

Another secondary loss that isn't normally named but that is commonly felt is the loss of self-confidence. With the loss of identity and purpose, on top of grief brain and shock, then trying to fill all the empty spaces that your person once occupied, you might feel totally disoriented.

Where you once considered yourself organized and competent—the type of person who gets her sh*t done—now, you are now wondering around like motherless Bambi.

You feel unsure of your surroundings and how to show up, which creates insecurity and self-doubt.

Where did this confident, self-assured person go?

I promise you, she is still there! She's simply adjusting to a brand-new environment. You've got to remember that your world has been shattered into one million pieces (who knows, maybe more?). You don't know how to operate in this new world yet, because you're still sorting out who you are and what matters. Your internal compass is pretty much gone.

So it makes total sense that you don't feel confident right now.

Confidence comes with repeated action.

You knew who you were and what mattered to you when your person was alive, and you lived that pattern out every day. Day after day after day you repeated many of the same behaviors and actions that built up a sense of self-confidence. With the old life behind you, you are basically starting from scratch.

You won't feel confident after someone you love dies. So instead of striving your confidence, I invite you to summon courage.

Courage is about bravery. It's about naming that this new terrain is foreign and scary, but finding the motivation within yourself to keep going.

Courage isn't the absence of fear; it's the acceptance of fear and taking action anyways.

You won't feel confident right now.

Strive for courage instead.

As you grieve and adapt to the loss of your person, in addition to all the other secondary losses that you are navigating, you might only be able to see the pain and discomfort (and that's okay!). My invitation is to also seek all the ways that you are also growing alongside your grief (even if it's a forced expansion).

The void is the invitation.

It's an ask from God, the universe, your inner knowing . . . maybe your deceased loved one to:

- Stretch your boundaries.
- Go beyond.
- Realize your potential.
- Do it anyways, even though it's hard . . . Because **you have a choice.** Your loved one didn't.

In the **grief** of their **death,** can you also see the **gift** of **life?**

Can you see the **end** of life as you knew it as a brand-new **beginning?**

These perspectives might feel stretchy—even activating! So if you feel the emotions starting to bubble beneath the surface, pay attention. Get curious about them. Ask them what wisdom they are trying to communicate, because they are your compass to areas of further healing and growth.

When one door of happiness closes, another opens;
but often we look so long at the closed door
that we do not see the one which has been opened for us.

—Helen Keller

Developing the Mindset to Move Forward

It is what it is

And

It will be what you make it.

Although it feels like you don't have much autonomy over your life right now, **you actually do!** And your ability to thrive in the aftermath of a loss is noticing where you have the power to exercise control, and also **where you don't.**

Your person died. You cannot change this. But you can change the tragic trajectory.

This is where mindset **comes into play!**

Some of you might not be ready to do this work. (And this is totally okay!) In early grief, the immense pain, sadness, and weight of a loss often blinds you from being able to take a step back and view your loss from a different perspective; one that doesn't solely paint the picture in darkness and tragedy.

So if these messages feel activating, just close this chapter for now and come back to it later. Grief changes. Just because you aren't ready at this second, doesn't mean you won't be later!

By now, we've covered how your beliefs about the world shape your thoughts, and your thoughts drive the way we feel. We've uncovered your old wounds and examined your childhood to understand where these beliefs and thoughts might have originated.

Mindset is about recognizing which beliefs serve you and changing the ones that don't.

So, let's get started by helping you identify the ones that don't.

Mindset Traps—the Three Ps

Psychologist Martin Seligman termed the Three Ps as critical component affecting resilience—meaning how we bounce back from hardship. The Three Ps—personalization, pervasiveness, and permanence—are limiting beliefs that are often experienced automatically (subconsciously), and arise when facing adversity. Once you understand what they are, you can notice if and when they come up for you, and stop yourself in the thought process.

Remember that breaking these negative thought cycles comes from practice! So for now, just focus on bringing awareness to your thoughts. As you read through each P, consider if you have felt this way in your grief.

#1 Personalization

The belief that the death was your fault. When you personalize your loss, you take the blame for it in some way. This could look like blaming yourself for allowing your kid to get into the car that was totaled by a drunk driver, or scouring through medical records wondering how you missed a symptom in the diagnosis that ended up terminal. Instead of accepting that other factors largely influence the outcome of these events, you might internalize problems or failures and hold yourself accountable. If you are personalizing your person's death, you might feel a lot of guilt and have trouble releasing it.

#2 Pervasiveness

The belief that the death will affect all areas of your life. I will admit that loss is pervasive as hell! It touches nearly every facet of your life. Pervasiveness becomes a threat to resilience when you proclaim that *everything in your life is awful* because your person died. You believe that the tragedy of your loss and heaviness of grief spans across all areas of your life, ruining literally every domain (work, hobbies, friendships, the food you used to eat, etc.). Again, your loss will *affect* these areas of your life—at work you might find it hard to focus, watching football without your dad might feel lonely. They will absolutely feel different, but they will not be spoiled forever.

You can challenge pervasiveness by noticing the areas of your life that still feel rewarding and worthwhile even after your loss. For me, that looked like finishing a challenging workout at the gym, going out with my girlfriends, or helping others heal with my business. I could still find value and joy in my life while I was grieving a major loss.

Tip: You might find that the activities that once felt worthwhile no longer feel so since your loss. If so, be open to trying to new ones!

#3 Permanence

The belief that the sorrow will last forever. I get it. When a loved one passes away the intensity and range of emotions makes it feel impossible to see a glimmer of light. You literally think that you will have to carry this heaviness for the rest of your life.

Permanence gives a name to this thought. It's the limiting belief that bad experiences or events last forever. Your mind can't comprehend that you are capable of changing this tragic trajectory, so you start feeling paralyzed and hopeless, causing even more overwhelm and panic, thus feeding the never-ending cycle. Instead of beating yourself up for feeling this way (I promise you, it's really common), just name it! Stop the cycle, validate how you are feeling, move that feeling or emotion through (see Part Two) and when you are calm and centered, remind yourself that the happiness, connection, love, and joy is coming—it's just not accessible to you YET!

Recognizing if and how the Three Ps are showing up in your grief journey and then changing the thoughts around these limiting beliefs can help re-instill a sense of hope and increase your resilience as you re-build your life.

Like I described in Part Two, *the facts of the death stay the same. But the story changes.* Your mindset shapes the way you perceive your story of loss. YOU control the narrative.

You already did some of the work to understand why you see your loss, your grief, death, and life at large the way you do by unpacking old wounds and examining conditioning and your family upbringing. In doing so **you can see**

how certain narratives aren't even yours! These are the ones you want to challenge and perhaps let go of, and to replace them instead with thoughts and beliefs that give your loss new meaning, so that you can integrate it.

Mindset supported me throughout my grief journey and still does to this day! What I'm teaching you builds the foundation for **consciousness,** which is basically noticing how your thoughts and beliefs shape your reality. It's your greater awareness about life and the world—the main ingredient that is needed to create a life where you don't just survive this loss, but **thrive!** Your journey to raised **consciousness** and becoming your highest self starts by recognizing that you have an abundance of choices when you start looking for the answers *within.*

So let's dive into some basic mindset shifts that you can apply in your grief.

Mindset Strategies

Use these strategies to help you shift your perspective on your grief and loss. Remember that this isn't just a clever trick to help you bypass your grief, it's an opportunity to try on a different narrative so that your brain can integrate this tragedy into your life.

Sliver Linings

This technique helps you look for the "good" in the "bad." Silver linings can help you create new meaning around your loss or other types of adversity.

For me, noticing how much I had grown as a result of my husband's death was a silver lining. Even though I didn't want my husband to die, I felt more grateful to be alive; I found myself more resilient having to rebuild a life without him; I took risks I never would have before, like sharing my story on social media and launching my own business. In his death, I was reborn—I was more awake to life. Looking for the good that came from the experience of loss didn't minimize the pain or tragedy of it—it softened it. Seeking the silver lining allowed me to integrate my husband's death into my life.

The Lesson

I truly believe that there are no real failures in life when you can extract the lesson from them. There is likely no lesson in your person's death, but there might be some in your experience of suffering and how you choose to live your life moving forward.

Ask yourself . . . *What can I learn from this experience? Knowing what I know now, what would I change about the way I live my life today?*

Or shift the question of *why did this happen TO me?* to *why did this happen FOR me?*

One of the biggest realizations I had after Ian's death was that the future is certainly not guaranteed. I thought that our dream of growing old together was promised. His passing spoke another truth. The lesson in losing my perfectly healthy thirty-two-year-old husband to cancer was that nothing in life is guaranteed! And as frightening as this all sounds, this lesson changed me! It allowed me to live more in the present and to worry less about the future. I've now learned how to make the most of today.

Reframing

This technique invites you to see something through another perspective, by looking for new angles. Small shifts can make a big impact here—for instance, reframing a current *problem* as a *challenge*. The subtle difference in language changes your entire perspective, and thus the approach or way of being in relation to the experience you're facing.

Here are some key steps to help you reframe toxic thoughts:

- **Catch it!** Notice when you are in the spiral of negative thought—*should-ing* on or criticizing yourself, or getting stuck in a limiting belief like one of the Three Ps.

- **Check it!** Yes, it's valid because you are feeling it, but *is the thought true?* Where is the evidence that you will feel this way forever? Is there another probable outcome—*like instead of living a life of misery and darkness after my loss, could another outcome be that I grow and re-build* *something stronger? Could I turn this pain into my purpose?* Sometimes it's easier to think of a friend who you are giving advice to instead of yourself! What would you say to them?

- **Change it!** Look for new angles and start to rewrite the narrative. I love coaching and grief groups for this because you have a lots of different perspectives in the room and one person to help you shift out of your limiting beliefs and negative thoughts.

You can start here by asking yourself:

- How can I see this through a different lens?
- Is there another angle here?
- How can I give it new meaning?

I struggled a lot with loneliness after Ian's death. After looking for the cure to my loneliness outside of myself—like distracting myself by dating, only to open myself to more heartbreak—I finally decided to look within! I got **curious** about loneliness and popped on Google for a quick search: "How to overcome loneliness?"

I learned that loneliness was described as the **pain** of being alone, while solitude was the **glory** of being alone.

Interesting! This finding enticed me because both loneliness and solitude were a product of being alone—but in one situation you felt pain, while in the other you felt glory. I realized that I could shift the way I was feeling lonely by changing my thoughts and beliefs around my alone time. I asked myself:

How can I learn to love my alone time?

How can I use this time to heal and discover new things about myself?

Why do I need to hear other people's voices instead of listening to mine?

When I realized that a lot of my loneliness had to do with simply getting used to taking up physical space alone, and the actual pain was more about grief, I used my alone time to heal! I shifted my loneliness into solitude by reframing by perspective on what it meant to be alone.

Reframing Death

Another powerful reframe that supported my healing, and that of many of my clients, has been changing the narrative around death. As I got **curious** about grief, I learned that my perspective on death was largely driven by societal conditioning. I realized how much entertainment, the taboo of speaking about death, and even popular holidays like Halloween, created fear around the subject.

Death had been positioned as something to be afraid of. It was dark, scary, and cast to the shadows. In movies and films, it was a sensationalized event to be beaten or outrun. Our culture had positioned death as the enemy and whoever is saved from it as the hero or heroine.

Uncovering this truth helped me reframe my perspective on death. I started seeing it as a natural passage. It was part of the cycle—deeply interconnected with life itself. Not only did this help me accept Ian's death, but it changed the way I viewed my life. By acknowledging death and accepting that our time here is finite, I could live with more gratitude and presence.

No one beats death. We *ALL* die! It's not a matter of *if*, but *when*.

Positive Affirmations and Mantras

These are statements or slogans that are repeated frequently to help you challenge and overcome self-sabotaging and negative thoughts. They can be spoken out loud, chanted, repeated in your head, or written on a sticky note and placed in a visible spot (my personal favorite). When you choose a mantra or positive affirmation, try to make it as authentic as possible by acknowledging where you are at. For example, I wouldn't suggest the affirmation of *Everything is awesome* after your person died, because clearly everything is not. You don't want to bypass the reality of your hardship, you want to rewire the negative thoughts (which starts by acknowledging them, first and foremost).

Keep in mind that some affirmations or mantras might feel a bit stretchy when you first start using them, but with time they drop in and become embodied. If you are rolling your eyes at the thought of sticky note supporting you through grief, I get it. Sounds kind of crazy, but these strategies do work! For now, I simply invite you to stay open-minded and try.

I felt incredibly broken as a widow. I believed I had baggage, that no one would ever desire me as I was wearing the scarlet letter of widow with two young kids attached at my hip. I didn't know who I was anymore or what I wanted out of my new life. I kept looking for ways to fill the void—launching an entirely new business, dating different guys, and exercising constantly—but nothing could fill my bottomless void.

My perspective started to shift after a yoga class one day, where lying in shavasana (corpse pose) the instructor offered the mantra . . .

I am enough.

I burst into tears. I didn't need another man. I didn't need more likes or followers! I didn't need the complete white-picket house and family. **I was already enough!** I wrote down this mantra in my journal and repeated it in my head as I lit a candle, turned on some music, and sat in silence before bed every night. I wrote it on sticky notes and pasted it to my computer screen—wherever I could it could, to reflect back my power.

Even in my state of brokenness, the mantra reminded me that I was full—I was complete and enough just being me.

Small Shifts in Language

Although this isn't an actual mindset technique, making small shifts in the language you use around grief and loss (by becoming more grief literate) can change a negative thought that is adding to your suffering. When you change the thought, you change the feeling—which allows you to relate to your grief and loss in a way that fosters healing and growth. Here are some examples:

* Moving ON to moving FORWARD.
* Why me? to what now?
* Why is this happening TO me? to why is this happening FOR me?

A NOTE ON TOXIC POSITIVITY

Beware of toxic positivity when applying these mindset techniques! These strategies aren't meant to bright-side or bypass the pain, they are meant to help you *integrate* it. So if a new perspective or silver lining doesn't feel true or in alignment, there's a chance it might be adding to your suffering instead of reducing it. There's a difference between stretching yourself to embody an aspirational concept versus totally dismissing your current grief and struggle.

Unfortunately, **you can't think your way out of grief**—I wish it was that easy— you have to FEEL it! Changing your mindset requires full alignment—with your body, mind, heart, and soul.

First and foremost, it's essential to validate (and feel) whatever feelings naturally arise for you in the grieving process and give yourself time to be with them. Once you've released them and are truly ready for a reframe, I invite you to consider the mindset strategies discussed here.

Duality

A key concept to prevent toxic positivity and minimize the guilt that typically arises when you start to look apply these mindset shifts is duality. Duality means that you can hold more than one emotion, feeling, belief, or even reality at a time. For example . . .

I can miss my past life that I shared with my husband AND feel excited about the new normal I am building without him.

I can love my late husband through the spiritual connection we share AND be in love with my new partner with whom I'm re-building a life now.

I can see Ian's death as a tragic ending AND as opportunity for rebirth, growth, and transformation.

In each of these, both statements are true!

Typically, when you're feeling a conflicting emotion and your mind tries to steer you in one direction or the other it forces you to decide between the two—*either/or*. This is because back in the caveman days you were surrounded by constant threats. Your mind had to make a quick decision—fight or flight—to get you out of harm's way, or you would be killed and eaten. Now we aren't under constant threat or attack, but our mind still works as though it is, so embracing duality can feel really hard.

In grief, there are many moments when conflicting emotions or realities arise simultaneously as you are grieving what was, embracing what is, and rebuilding what will be (as displayed in the Dual Process Model of Coping with Bereavement on page 87). So instead of trying to choose between only grief or only moving forward, duality gives you the option to hold the feelings and beliefs of **both realities!**

You can feel profound longing and sadness that your loved one is gone AND deep gratitude for being alive, followed by excitement and passion to make the most of it.

Resilience

The work that you are doing right now—learning about grief, reading this book, embracing duality, and trying on different perspectives to find meaning in all of this—form the building blocks of resilience.

Resilience is your ability to "bounce back" and/or recover quickly from difficulty. It's the strength and speed of your response to adversity. In terms of what you are currently navigating, it's the process of adapting well to a life-altering loss that fundamentally changes you from the inside out.

With grief and trauma, people fall within one of three groups related to resilience:

- Those who don't bounce back.
- Those who bounce back.
- Those who bounce back stronger (pssst—this is post-traumatic growth!).

So why would some people come back from this stronger while others don't bounce back at all? Is it because resilience only comes naturally to some of us but not to others? Are you simply born more resilient?

The answer is no. **Resilience isn't fixed.** In fact, resilience can be developed and built by:

* Increasing your self-awareness.
* Understanding your beliefs about the world and what drives them.
* Exploring how you deal with conflict, failure, pain, and hardship.
* Making a change and continuing to repeat the change to create a habit.

This cycle increases neuroplasticity, which is the ability of your brain to rewire itself. So if you don't feel resilient now, keep going! You can absolutely strengthen this muscle.

Now, some people have been raised in situations where resilience flourishes more than others. If you had a parental figure who instilled a sense of confidence by telling you, *Emily, you can do anything you put your mind to!*, the foundations of resilience have already been laid. Factors that affect resilience include support, finances, cultural beliefs, and family upbringing (having a healthy attachment and someone who believes in you), past (and current) trauma, mindset and religion/faith/spirituality. Basically, all of the factors that we covered in Part Two that can also add to your suffering while grieving.

Reality check:

Not everyone will rise from the ashes.

Not everyone will grow through their grief.

But what I hope you gain from reading this section is that **growth, transformation, and truly thriving after loss is possible!** And there are tools accessible to everyone to get you there.

You might not believe in yourself right now—again, because your confidence is shot! So instead, can you summon some courage?

Can you walk *with* the fear and uncertainty and begin to envision a future that looks just a bit brighter that this?

You with me? Let's go!

Imagination and Hope

Imagination is our ability to see beyond "what is." It's the capacity of our mind to get creative or resourceful to envision something that doesn't exist yet.

When Ian died, I'd have friends approach me and say, *I'm so sorry for your loss, Emily. I just can't imagine what you're going through.*

I thought, *of course you can't imagine this! And why would you want to?* At first, their inability to see me (or even try to) was infuriating. But it also got me thinking about how key imagination is to the grieving process.

When you are in the thick of devastation and despair. When your entire world has been shattered. When all you see in the distant future is a vast, blank slate. **Imagination is key to moving forward.** It's your ability to see beyond the present wreckage—to splash a dash of paint on the blank canvas—and trust that some type of formation (maybe one day a masterpiece) will come to fruition!

Imagination takes courage—doing it even though you're scared. Imagination takes creativity—seeing your situation through a different lens. Imagination takes vision—venturing into the unknown and flirting with uncertainty.

In order to start imagining and tapping into the realm of possibility and desire, you first have to access hope. HOPE is a feeling of expectation or desire for a certain thing to happen. It's the belief in yourself—trusting in your own capabilities and strength.

Hope helps you see the light in darkest of moments—even if it's just a glimmer—and inspires you to keep going in the face of fear, doubt, and uncertainty.

Imagination is absolutely critical to the quality of our lives.
Our imagination enables us to leave our routine everyday existence
by fantasizing about travel, food, sex, falling in love,
or having the last word—all the things that make life interesting.
Imagination gives us the opportunity to envision new possibilities—
it is an essential launchpad for making our hopes come true.
It fires our creativity, relieves our boredom, alleviates our pain,
enhances our pleasure, and enriches our most intimate relationships.

—Bessel van der Kolk, *The Body Keeps the Score*

Every emotion stems from either fear or desire. In grief, almost everything you are feeling is fear-based. So in order to restore balance and walk *with* fear, you have to equally build up your desire. Your sheer will to LIVE in the face of death!

Hope, imagination and vision fuel the flames of desire. And in order to thrive in life after loss, your desire has to be greater than your fear.

So this is my invitation to start seeking the light. Find the glimmers of hope and evidence that you are capable of. Don't wait until you feel confident or ready—because you likely will not ever be.

Remember that you've already walked yourself through the worst of it and you are stronger and more resilient for it.

Part Four

Thrive

✤

The death of a loved one
burns your entire life down.
Like a phoenix, may you rise
more enlightened, resilient,
and grateful, knowing
what it means to die
and choosing to live fully
amid the ashes.

Six months after Ian's death I started asking myself . . . **what now?**

Rebuilding a life without my husband felt intimating AF, and the blank slate of the future gave me no clear direction where I should even start. **What was I going to do with my life?** I needed to make money, but I also needed flexibility to be able to raise my kids as a solo mom. My nine-to-five job would pay the bills, but it didn't fit the demands of my life outside the office, nor did it light me up.

The experience of Ian's death had changed me—**the things that used to matter simply didn't anymore.**

I had watched my once-strong, athletic, healthy husband fade away into the shell of a human being. I had witnessed him fighting excruciating pain just to play with our kids, or on some days, barely get out of bed. I had faced death head on and seen my own mortality, thus **I felt more grateful to be alive!**

As I was grieving all that I had **lost,** and simultaneously I was more aware of what I still **had.**

For one, I had been blessed with the liberty of choice—to simply **be** here! Ian didn't get that choice. He was forced to surrender. And after watching him fight like a warrior to survive, I felt like I owed it to him to make the most of the time I had here.

This deep appreciation for life **opened up new possibilities for me!**

I wanted to create an impact in my limited time here.

I wanted to honor Ian and extend his impact here on Earth.

I wanted to create a legacy not just for him, but also for **myself!**

So I started to get curious about my path forward.

When Ian was receiving cancer treatments, I had been sharing updates about our journey on a GoFundMe to cover medical expenses. After his death, friends and family asked me if I'd continue to write. They commented on my way with words and said my posts changed their perspectives on their own life . . . for the better. In addition to their encouraging words, writing was extremely therapeutic for me. So as a **baby step** forward, I decided to start a blog and share my story on social media.

Immediately, I was connected to thousands of other young widows who "got me." Where I once felt isolated and almost victimized in my immediate circle of friends, I now had an instant **community** to navigate my loss with. These strangers on the internet viscerally knew my struggles. They shared how my words helped them feel seen and validated in their experience of loss, and with every comment or like of a post they helped me feel seen and validated in mine.

Their feedback was alchemy for my broken heart, which ignited the initial idea to transform my pain into purpose. By helping others with my experience of loss, Ian's death started to take on a whole new **meaning.**

My story of tragedy became one hope for others.

The seeds for my future vision had been planted, but I wasn't sure yet what I wanted to grow. So through a series of synchronicities I hired goal coach Jacki Carr to help me to cultivate my idea. She introduced me to core values work, which helped me connect back to myself by defining **what mattered to me now.** My core values became my internal compass to guide me down the path of alignment and truth.

As I was figuring out my purpose, I was also getting to know my **SELF.** I felt like I didn't know who I was anymore after parts of my identity died with Ian. So I studied archetypes, the Enneagram, and even paid for an astrological birth chart reading to find out more. By getting **curious** about who I was at my essence, I started to realize that I had unique gifts that **I was meant to share and bring forward into this world.**

All of the evidence outside of me supported the findings that I was discovering about myself within, but there were parts of me that still felt afraid to follow my calling. I started to doubt myself, "Who was I to help others navigate their loss when I was barely surviving myself?".

I also faced criticism from family: "Why was I wasting time starting a blog when I had kids to raise? Their father died, they had no one else but me."

I started to second-guess it all . . . "Was I just being selfish?"

In times where the fear and insecurities started to speak louder than my desire to follow my little voice within, **I asked Ian for advice.** I would sit out on the porch at night and look out at the stars, or just lie in bed and close my eyes . . . and he'd respond! It wasn't a loud and clear answer—but I could hear his voice in my heart and through our endless love telling me to **go for it.** To follow my intuition, to take the leap, and become the entrepreneur he had always encouraged me to be.

So I listened.

Through my core values work, guidance from my mentor Jacki, my research into SELF, validation from Ian, and starting to trust that I was perhaps meant to inspire others to find light in the darkness . . .

move*THRU* was born!

I honestly didn't care if the business succeeded or failed! I had a roof over my head and was financially safe for at least a year. What mattered to me was getting my story out there.

To create a movement.

To inspire others to move through the pain.

To discover that life doesn't end after a loved one's death. It begins!

I didn't have a detailed business plan or even a clear vision of what the future would look like. I probably had a million reasons not to take the leap, but **my desire** to create impact, to honor Ian's legacy, and to heal my broken heart **was bigger than any fear** stopping me.

As much as I wanted evidence that everything would work out, I simply trusted that if it didn't, I'd be able to be solution-oriented and figure it out. If I needed evidence, I would reflect on everything I had just walked myself through . . .

A fifteen-month cancer battle.

Watching my husband pass away before me.

Surviving the early months of grief—solo parenting and being on my own.

And I thought to myself . . . I've got this!

My experience of loss—of suffering and deep pain—had given me something I didn't anticipate.

It gave me grit . . .

It gave me courage, and . . .

It gave me deep sense of trust in MYSELF. I had walked myself through fire.

I was FIREPROOF.

Moving Forward with Meaning

Using my story of loss to help other grievers feel seen, validated, and empowered in theirs, gave Ian's death new meaning. It didn't take away the hurt of losing him, but it softened it. The new meaning gave me something other than just pain and tragedy to hold on to—it was my lifeline keeping me afloat. Without it, I was left drowning in darkness.

Human beings are meaning-making machines. It's our brain's way of making sense of the people, places, and the events that occur in our lives—connecting them all together to instantaneously create a story.

Think of a time when you were dating. Maybe you've been texting for a month now and you just came off a hot date. You send a text to check-in and are met with no response. You keep checking your phone . . .

That's strange. Usually he texts back right away. I wonder if everything is okay?

Another hour goes by.

Maybe he got in an accident!

Or wait, NO! . . . Is he on another date?

I guess he's just not that into me after all.

And so the story continues.

Instead of allowing the answers to unfold in due time, your brain feels this urgency to connect all the dots! It sucks at being in the gray area or dancing in the limbo of uncertainty, so it creates a plot line to give us a sense of control.

When it comes to your person's death, your brain goes into hyperdrive trying to make sense of this seismic shift that has occurred in your life. Imagine a little writer in your head feverishly typing away at the latest breaking news in your life and speculating into the future of what this might all mean for you. What this writer is trying to do is **integrate** your person's death.

The next phase of healing and growth—of thriving after a loss—is learning how to control that little voice. This is **consciousness.** And there's nothing like a life-altering loss to break you wide open and make you aware of all the subconscious thoughts, beliefs, and layers of conditioning that massively influence your lived reality!

Until you make the unconscious conscious,
it will direct your life and you will call it fate. —Carl Jung

Facts vs. Stories

Since Ian's death, my story of loss has changed from one of tragedy and darkness to one of survival and light. I've learned that **I control the narrative** around my loss, and my story continues to evolve with each new chapter I write.

You've started to separate the facts of the death from your story, by bringing **conscious** awareness to your thought patterns and understanding where they originate (see Part Two). The more you untangle these beliefs from your lived reality, the more you control the narrative.

You can give your loss whatever meaning you want!

Meaning-making

It's hard to find meaning or look for themes beyond the pain and suffering when you are in deep grief. To get to meaning, you have to move through the pain. It takes time and continuously evolves, so **honor wherever you are in your journey.**

Meaning doesn't take away the pain, nor does it give a reason to a death. In general, death is meaningless—it's unpredictable and random—often making no sense at all.

For instance, I'll never have a "reason" for why my thirty-two-year-old perfectly healthy husband got diagnosed with cancer and died. *I guess I could boil it down to bad genes?* Regardless, you will never be satisfied with the reason or why.

The meaning is in you. It's how you perceive the loss and integrate it into your life. It's how you make sense of it all through whatever story *you* choose to write!

Meaning-making helps you further integrate the loss, make peace with the pain, and move forward as you carry your loved one with you. They will forever be a leading character in your story of life.

How to Find Meaning

Meaning-making isn't a clever reframe or silver lining—those are just *tools* to help you get there! Meaning making doesn't have to be a big event or grand gesture, like starting a foundation or cause, it can be as simple as feeling changed by your person or choosing to live your life in a way that they would be proud.

To find meaning and *feel* its truth flowing through your entire body and soul, start small. **Seek it from within.** Notice the moments of where you feel love and gratitude mixed in with the pain. Search for it in your heart—where grief and love meld as one.

Toolkit to Find Meaning

Here are some subtle ways that you can begin looking for new angels beyond the pain and suffering, to give your loss new meaning:

- Find gratitude for the time you had with your loved one.

- Explore ways to commemorate and honor your deceased person.

- Notice if and how you feel changed by knowing your person.

- Notice if and how you feel changed by their death.

- Try creating something of meaning for others.

- Recognize the fragility or value of life and make changes to how you prioritize your time.

- Seek the good in the bad and find ways to carry both (duality).

- Find the lessons from your experience of loss and allow them to guide you, moving forward.

- Take ownership and trust that you control the narrative of your story.

- Reinvest emotional energy into new people, new goals, new identity, and purpose in life.

Meaning-making is highly personal and unique to each griever. For now, get **curious** about it, stay open-minded and simply follow your heart. Trust that beneath all the layers of pain that you are moving through, you will access the love.

Reclaiming Your Life through Consciousness

Let's return to that long dirt road.

There you are standing right in the middle between the life that *was* and the life that *will be*. You want to move forward, but you aren't sure how. It's like you're literally starting over—and there are so many paths forward to choose from.

Many grievers will take **the path that feels familiar.** It's reminiscent of your old life, which feels comforting and nostalgic. So you decide to go back to your nine-to-five job—it's safe, predictable, and comfortable. *My needs are met, my kids are provided for—I've got this!* But after a couple months, the work feels stale. You might connect with old friends, work around the house, or pick up a hobby or two, but nothing seems to light you up. The things that mattered to you before seem flat or immaterial, but you're safe and comfortable, which is enough.

Another group of grievers will take **the path that feels uncertain . . . but alive!** This direction feels magnetic. You don't know what's there for you, but you can't help but follow the call.

There's an energy, an allure—a vibration—that's begging you to tap into and let it play out.

This road feels risky and nostalgic all at the same time. It's like a wild whisper that you've never heard (or maybe just didn't listen to) that's inviting you back home.

This road is the path of your **intuition!** It's where your passions, desires, and dreams come alive. You've heard their calling before, but the hustle culture, limiting beliefs, fears, and conditioning of society spoke louder.

But now, in the wake of devastation and darkness, you are listening.

These voices are your compass to what's next. They are guiding you back home—to who you are at your essence **(your identity!)** and what you want to do in this finite time here on Earth called life **(your purpose!).**

So let's learn how to listen to their subtle whispers.

You can look at the blank slate of the future with fear or . . . With the excitement and possibility to create whatever you want.

Discovering Your Identity: WHO YOU ARE

Remember that sliver I showed you in Part Three? This is the version of you post-loss. There are still pieces of the *old* version of you—the you in relation to your person—but there is a big carved-out section of you that is missing. These parts of your identity died with your person, so it *feels* like a piece of you is gone.

This feeling describes the **death of identity.**

As disorienting and painful as this rupture can be, it's also an invitation to go deep within and truly meet yourself at your essence; beyond the ego roles or the societal boxes you used to check, and beneath the formations that your ancestral patterns, conditioning, and family upbringing shaped you to be.

Identity is who you are. The search for identity after a loss is less about *finding* yourself again, more about *remembering.*

At birth, you were like clay. Before you could walk or talk your parents started to shape you. And they did this accordingly to how their parents shaped them. Their beliefs about what type of sculpture they would mold you into were informed by generations before them, societal norms, religious and cultural beliefs, and past traumas (are you starting to see a theme here?).

You might have been raised in a home where your unique gifts and talents were **celebrated** and **fostered.** Maybe you were super expressive—you loved dressing up and dancing around as your parents filmed you on camera. Your parents or support figures encouraged this vivacious energy and helped you embrace this innate part of yourself. So as an adult you identified with being animated, fun-loving, entertaining, and enthusiastic. This was part of your identity.

Or maybe you were raised in a home where your unique gifts and talents were **shunned** and **suppressed.** Maybe this expressive young girl was reprimanded for acting silly—she was being too loud or too much. Your parents or support figures discouraged this playful energy and scolded you for not doing something more responsible or academic. This innate part of yourself was cast into the shadows. So as an adult you identify with being serious, refined, and responsible—but these traits don't really **feel** like **YOU.** There's an entirely different side to yourself that hasn't been developed but that feels so true!

So how do you come back to YOU? How do you remember who you are?

Check out the toolkit for some ideas to un-become you and to return to you.

Toolkit to Discover Your Identity

Here are some ways that you can remember yourself at your essence to find your true identity.

Therapy

Honestly, I can't emphasize enough how much therapy has raised my consciousness and allowed me to tap into the truth of who I am. Going back into your childhood and seeing all of the ways by which you've been conditioned, shaped, and molded by outside forces is really revealing—and admittedly painful at times. That's why I recommend consulting a professional who can hold that container for you and help you process everything that's coming up.

If you don't want to dig (or aren't ready to—and believe me, I 100 percent respect that). You can start with the tool below to get a sense of who you have always been, but not dig into potential old wounds.

Enneagram

The Enneagram is a dynamic system of nine personality types that describe patterns in how people interpret the world and manage their emotions. There is one personality that typically stands out from the rest, which is called your "core type." This type was likely developed through childhood. You can use the Enneagram to understand yourself and others better, by bringing awareness to what motivates you and the lenses through which you will filter your new world. The Enneagram helps you uncover your internal wiring, your base fear and base desire, as well as your unconscious and conscious motivations.

I use this tool in my grief groups to help clients better understand their identity and validate their unique needs for grief—because everyone grieves differently and your Enneagram type helps inform this.

You can take the official test to find out what type you are by visiting The Enneagram Institute at enneagraminstitute.com.

Here are some other tools to explore to help you get a sense of who you are: Human Design, Myers-Briggs Type Indicator, and an astrological birth chart reading.

Discovering Your Purpose: WHAT YOU DO

Purpose is a function of doing. It's what you do in life to make an impact or a difference. Some of us find a deep sense of purpose in staying at home to raise kids, while others find fulfillment shining on a big stage, sharing words of hope and inspiration. Some find their purpose diving into data and making sense of patterns, while others find meaning in applying that science in real time, through curing patients in hospital beds.

Your purpose refers to what you want to achieve in this lifetime! It's made up of all the different people, places, and pursuits that add to the significance of life.

Your person was likely a big part of your purpose; he or she as a person and all the activities you did together added meaning and richness to your life. In the wake of your person's death, you were left with this massive void. Some of this space you were *forced* to fill on your own. Maybe you had to figure out how to raise the kids solo, to fix appliances by yourself, to make financial decisions independently, and assume new roles and responsibilities in order to simply keep moving forward with life.

As you filled the void, you stretched and grew! And doing so, **your core beliefs about the world and how you want to show up in it might have shifted.** This is the integrated version of you—the 2.0, post-traumatic, growth side of SELF who has walked herself through fire and is now FIREPROOF.

Okay, maybe you don't feel that way yet . . . but maybe after this chapter you'll start to see that as a possibility?!

Your experience of loss, grief, suffering, and surviving has fundamentally changed who you are and what matters to you! You might have already started to notice and feel these changes when we learned about post-traumatic growth in Part Three. You know now more than ever that your time here is limited, but you also don't know what to do with it. You want to find your purpose, but you don't quite know how.

It's normal to look for these answers *outside* of yourself—to discover what's deemed worthy by societal standards, to take the advice from your parents or whatever fits inside another cultural norm. But instead, I invite you to look *within*. Access your internal compass to guide you down the next path. This is the path of alignment and truth—where meaning, significance, richness, and boundless love coincide.

This is your path to thriving in life after loss. Here are some tools to get started!

Toolkit to Discover Your Purpose

Your core values are your belief system. They signify what's important to you— **what matters.**

Think of them as your internal GPS, providing you with direction in life to guide you down the path of purpose. When you live in alignment with your core values you feel at ease and in flow. Everything that you do feels meaningful and rich!

To determine your core values, try this exercise that my mentor Jacki Carr taught me when I was trying to figure out my next steps in life after loss:

- Search for a list of core values online.
- Circle ten core values that feel like home. These should be words that you feel anchored in—that feel like your truth. These should not be words that you aspire to be!
- After you have ten, cut this list in half—circle five that feel the most true and centered like your core.
- After you have these five words, define them for yourself. If you circled *freedom*, what does that mean to you? If you circled *creativity*, write down your definition.
- Consider sharing your core values with a friend or family member, and ask them if they feel true to you.
- Then reflect on how you are living in alignment with your core values, or, more revealing, are not! Make shifts accordingly.

Remember that your core values have likely changed since your person's death, and they might keep changing as you continually grow and evolve.

Lessons from Loss

As we discussed in Part Two, you might feel changed by the experience of loss. There are many lessons or insights that can only be achieved in hindsight, when it's too late. A beautiful way to find healing and closure in life after loss is to name the lessons you have learned from this experience, and set up your life to intentionally live in accordance with them.

Consider the questions below and take time to reflect and journal about them.

- How has my experience of loss changed me?
- What do I know to be true about myself and the world around me now?
- What do I know now that I wish I had known before my person died?
- How would I have lived my life differently knowing what I know now?
- How can I apply these lessons to inform the way I live my life moving forward?

Here is a list of common lessons and insights that might prompt further inquiry:

- Not working so hard.
- Making space for quality time with friends and family.
- Being more mindful.
- Finding the answers within.
- Not being afraid of risk, challenge, pain, or uncertainty.
- Taking less for granted.
- Living more fully in alignment with *your* truth (not that of others).
- Finding gratitude in the small things.
- Making peace with the natural endings in life.
- Learning to live in the questions.

Keep going with this practice! You might be surprised at how much you've learned from your experience of this. Then use some of these lessons to guide you down your path forward. If a big lesson was not being afraid to take a risk because tomorrow isn't guaranteed, then buy the plane ticket—take the trip!

Follow Your Passion

I often see clients get frustrated or stuck when their purpose doesn't appear loud and clear. This is totally normal, because, again, your entire world has shifted! So I invite you to take this work a little less seriously by sprinkling in some playfulness and curiosity. Your passions—the hobbies and interests that you naturally gravitate toward—are the subtle whispers of your soul saying, "Pay attention! I want you to take me **there**." Don't underestimate their validity! These voices are guiding you to your purpose—they are the stepping stones. Your job is to get quiet and listen.

Passion Exercise

This one is super easy! All you need to do is grab a pen and paper and write down what lights you up. Make a list of your passions, your hobbies, and any activities that bring you joy. Your excitement is the inner validation that you need to stop looking for permission outside of yourself!

So . . .

- Make the list.
- Carve out time to do one or two activities on your list, and
- GET OUT THERE AND DO IT!

Other questions for reflection:

- What do your friends come to you for?
- What do they think you are "good" at?
- Have you been recognized for your skills or accomplishments in a certain area?

These questions aren't about external validation but to reflect what we often fail to see in ourselves.

All of these tools help you to look within for the answers. They help you connect back to your intuition to guide you down the next path.

Excitement is life energy begging to be played out. Listen to it.

Allow it to guide you to your purpose.

Your Purpose Doesn't Have to Be So BIG!

It's quite common in our society, for **purpose** to get highly externalized or monetized. We associate purpose with outside measures of success like the car you drive, your job title, dollars in the bank, or social media likes and followers. We attach purpose to an outcome when in reality there is purpose simply in your presence—*in simply being!*

So when you are searching for your purpose, notice if and when you tie it to an outcome. **Your purpose doesn't have to be loud and proud, monetized, or even material** . . . it can be something much more subtle, but still feel extremely alive for you.

Here are some more intrinsic-centered activities that might align with your purpose:

- Making deep and meaningful connections by spending time with family and friends.

- Researching a topic out of the pure pleasure that it brings you to learn about something new.

- Helping others in need by volunteering for a cause you are passionate about.

- Creating beauty by decorating your home or tending to a garden, tree, or plants.

- Coaching a team and teaching them new skills and character traits.

What are some of the more subtle activities that give you intrinsic meaning?

Your Next Chapter

Despite how called I felt to share my story of loss and start move*THRU*, I still had the voices of fear, self-doubt, and judgment creep in and try to persuade me otherwise. This is where I really had to double-down on my desire—fueling it by tapping into the realm of possibility; and where I learned to silence the outside noises, rewrite my limiting beliefs, and dance in the magic of uncertainty.

When my mind tried to convince me of all the reasons not to, I tapped into my body and deep within my heart—where I could better hear my intuition. This is the place from where I took action . . .

If it felt good, I was two feet in!

Fear is stored in your mind,

Intuition is stored in your body.

As you begin to remember your true *self* and figure out what you want to do with this precious time here, you start to question how you will actually put these ideas into action. How do you bring them to life?

Maybe you truly desire to start the foundation in honor of your loved one, or share your story on social media to help others heal. You feel the pull at your heartstrings, the excitement begging to be played out, and vision starting to unfold. But just as you get ready to put pen to paper and draw out that vision board, another voice enters . . .

Who am I to do this?

What will they think of me? There's just way too much risk.

Cue all the limiting beliefs, self-doubts, judgments, and fears.

These thoughts are normal and they arise to protect us. Your mind is wired to keep you out of harm's way. So your fears are ultimately a form a *protection*. But fears also *prevent* you from taking action on your purpose—on what actually matters to you. So instead of doing the thing that feels aligned and meaningful, fear persuades you to play it safe.

Toolkit to Walk WITH Fear

The reality is that you won't eliminate fear—your brain is literally wired for it! It perceives *same* as safe and *different* as a threat; hence, why we are so afraid of change!

So, even if you are miserable in your current situation, your brain might still favor what's *familiar* over a *new possibility*, despite its potential to bring positive change to your life. That's why we have to train our brains (i.e., mindset) to be open to change and taking a risk.

Here are some strategies that can help.

Fuel Your Desire

In order to take action on your purpose, **your desire has to be greater than your fear.** Your brain is predisposed to *worst*-case-scenario thinking because of your brain's built-in survival response, so you can alchemize that fear by switching to *best*-case scenario thinking!

Play with the potential ways in which your life could be changed *for the better* by taking action on what matters to you. Maybe it's getting to spend more time with your kids, having the freedom to work from anywhere in the world, or expressing yourself in way that feels authentic and true.

Take a few moments to write down the best-case scenario.

If I were to act on my purpose, how might this actually work?

How could my life actually be changed for the better?

Access Safety and Trust Within

YOU are your safest asset.

It's not the job you hold or the money in your bank account. These are just projections of freedom, security, and control. Our brain thinks we need these material things to protect our liberty and keep us safe, but the reality is that in a world of chaos and uncertainty, you've got to access trust and safety from within.

How? Look for evidence of times that you already have!

Remind yourself that nothing prepared you for the loss of your loved one. **See** how solution-oriented you moved through tragedy despite having all the answers. **Remember** the resilience and grit you accessed to redirect and rise.

You are more prepared now than ever to handle whatever life throws your way, so recollect just how powerful you are.

Change Your Relationship with the Unknown

Humans don't like uncertainty. We typically thrive in safety, predictability, and situations that give us a sense of control. What I've realized after Ian's death, however, is that there is no certainty in life. **All we can control is our response to uncertainty.**

So instead of trying to fight the uncertainty, I invite you to **change your relationship with it.**

Ask yourself . . .

- Can I tap into the magic of not knowing, and by allowing myself to be curious, stay open, and be surprised by what naturally unfolds?
- Can I ride the excitement and anticipation of the plot line as it gradually builds and adapt as it twists and turns without needing to know the ending?
- Can I take action out of pure motivation from how good it feels, how much joy it brings me right now without attaching my decision to a future outcome?
- Can I live in the questions and allow the answers to materialize, trusting that there is lesson in everything?

Control is an illusion. You know firsthand that nothing—not even tomorrow—is guaranteed.

So notice when your brain sends you into a fear spiral trying to name all the ways it won't work out or plan every detail to protect you from failure. This is false protection!

Do what makes you feel the most alive—what brings you the most joy—right here. Right now.

Toolkit to Overcome Doubts and Judgments

Think back to your childhood.

Maybe you always had a fascination with the moon and the stars. You dreamed of blasting off into outer space to explore galaxies and discover new life on foreign planets. You geeked out on everything science, astrology, and space travels. So one day, you summoned up the courage to tell your parents that you wanted to become an astronaut when you grew up, and instead of meeting you with shared excitement and enthusiasm, they told you . . .

I don't think so buddy. That's not a practical job. How about accounting instead?

You didn't know it at the time, but their response made an imprint. It spurred the belief that your dreams aren't trustworthy, that risk is not safe, and that practicality and security should be prioritized over chasing your passions in life.

These seemingly insignificant events that we experience throughout our childhood and into adulthood create limiting beliefs. A limiting belief is a thought that was initially meant to *protect* you but is now *persecuting* you because it's blocking you from acting out of false defense. Limiting beliefs are driven by fear, protecting you from the pain of disappointment, rejection, shame, or failure that comes with living your truth.

At some point you were being yourself. Then someone told you that you were *too much, it wasn't practical, that's not appropriate,* or worse . . . *you are no longer welcome here* . . . so you changed your behavior. You started being less. You began to conform. You stopped dreaming to avoid the hurt.

So now, the same beliefs that were there to keep you safe are essentially sabotaging you from realizing your purpose.

The way to rewrite your limiting beliefs is to:

Name them. Write them down.

I don't have the credentials.

I'm not inspiring enough.

I don't want to look stupid.

Get curious about them. Ask yourself why you feel this way about yourself. Keep asking yourself why until you get to the root cause—the origin of the thought.

Challenge and rewrite the root thought. Ask yourself, is this true? Maybe it's true for you but what about the broader population? Does it hold up?

Even a short twenty minutes spent reflecting on your childhood will bring an awareness to your limiting beliefs—why it's easier for some people to blast off to the moon, and why for others they will never launch.

Reframe Judgments from Others

I hear this one come up all the time:

What will my in-laws think of me?

My friends don't seem to get why this matters to me.

Unfortunately, not too many people will. The exact thing that scares you also scares them. But here you are summoning the courage to do it anyway. You know what this does? It activates them! You jumping two feet in to follow your heart and purpose triggers their inability to do so themselves. You are a mirror of everything they are not. So you living your purpose subconsciously brings up feelings of disappointment, failure, and shame for them.

Relationships are like mirrors; you reflect back the insecurities of others, while they reflect back yours. So when you feel like someone is judging you for grieving wrong, or dating too soon, or quitting your job to take the bucket-list trip of a lifetime, it's not their judgment that's stopping you. It's your own.

To release these judgments:

See everyone in your life as a mirror.

If you don't like the reflection, look *within* (remember, it's not them, it's you!).

Make peace with and heal whatever you are worried about them thinking of you, because ultimately this is what you think of yourself.

Connect to Your Why

Your why is the motivation driving your big life change. It's the energy behind the action of all the things that you do that bring meaning and purpose into your life.

If it's working less to spend more time with your family, your why might be freedom and making meaningful connections.

If it's starting a community garden in your neighborhood, your why might be to make the world more beautiful or for the pure enjoyment and degree of presence you get while sinking your hands in the dirt.

If it's organizing an advocacy walk, your why might be to raise awareness about your person's illness and honor their legacy, which helps you maintain your relationship with them.

Your why is what keeps you going when times get tough, when the fears, the doubts, and judgments from others start to close in. If you're wobbly on your why, those voices will win and you'll find yourself living someone else's truth instead of your own.

If you have an idea percolating, I invite you to get crystal clear on your why. Reflect on the following:

What is my idea?

Why do I want to do this? Think in terms of the impact you will create (such as helping others to heal) and what benefits this change adds to your life (more freedom, more time with friends, etc.).

Your why is the fuel that ignites the fires of change. You've got to build the heat in order to make the jump!

Stop Thinking. Start Doing.

Because you brain is literally wired to protect you, it will think of a million reasons why you should not act on your new-found calling. You might have all the awareness around your limiting beliefs and self-judgments, but you won't rewrite them by *thinking* about your purpose. **You'll rewrite them by acting on it!**

Whatever idea you decide to bring to life—maybe it's sharing that first social media post about your story of loss—you won't feel confident or sure of your decision in the beginning.

Remember, confidence takes repeated action! So you build evidence for your nervous system by:

1. Committing to do the thing, then
2. Following through.

When you follow through on a commitment, you're telling your subconscious that you are reliable and trustworthy. This reinforces your decision to shake things up and create change, so that you can bring meaning and purpose to your life.

So ask yourself, what is one small thing I can do to move me closer to manifesting my purpose? Write it down.

Now, schedule time in your calendar to actually **go do it.**

Then, do it again!

Consistency and repetition are key here. YOLO friends!

*If you can't do it for **you**. Do it for **them**.*

They didn't have a choice. You do.

Thriving in Life after Loss

So what does it mean to thrive?

Webster gives us the following definitions . . .

- To prosper
- To do well
- To flourish
- To grow vigorously
- To be successful

What does thriving mean to you? Define what it means to prosper. What is your definition of success? What would flourishing look like?

To me . . . thriving means living in alignment with your truth.

When you live in alignment with **who you are** and **what matters to you,** it feels like you're sailing along with the current of life instead of fighting it. Your inherent gifts and strengths are maximized, which fosters competence and pride in everything you do. You believe that you actually have a divine talent, which releases the pressure of trying to be something that you're not. This helps you accept others' differences as well, by knowing that we all fit together like puzzle pieces in the greater game of life.

When you do more of what matters—acting on your purpose—you feel more fulfilled. Life breathes richness and deep meaning, which adds new dimensions to your life. You aren't just shuffling papers around your office on auto drive because your boss told you to; you are crystal clear on your why, living in full alignment and motivated by the freedom, adventure, quality time, and presence you get from doing something you love.

Living in alignment with your truth demands awakening your **consciousness.** And there's nothing like a life-altering loss to break you wide open to unearth these beliefs about yourself and the world.

Consciousness is key because it grants you freedom. It allows you to dance outside of the 3D realm where choices are limited, and into the 4D (your inner world) all the way to the 5D (the unseen), where possibilities are endless!

You might not have known it, but you've been playing in the 4D and dipped your toes into the 5D since you started reading this book. Further, I want to note that there are many definitions of these realms, but I'm interpreting them through the lens of grief and life after loss.

The 3D: Your Physical World

It's really hard to thrive after a loss if you're only living in 3D. It's here that your emotions are labeled as good or bad. Your person's death holds only one meaning: tragedy. You are a victim of your circumstance because you believe that no one else suffers; and your life is headed toward gloom and doom because it no longer meets the societal standards of success.

While it's hard to thrive under these conditions, there's a lot of growth that happens in the 3D. This is your *physical* world, so all the ways by which you've filled the void and adapted to life without your person take place here. In the 3D, you've become more resilient, you've grown alongside your grief, and perhaps you've started to see new possibilities in life, which propel you into the 4D.

The 4D: Your Inner World

The 4D is your gateway to the 5D. This is where you enter another realm by becoming an *observer* of your experience of loss. You start to notice the subtle voices within and understand the power of your thoughts—how that might be adding to your suffering (Part Two) or your ability to survive. You begin to release the charge around your emotions, notice the stories you are creating, and understand that you are in charge of the narrative!

In the 4D you begin to see that you are the creator of your own reality. You can change the meaning of any situation by seeking an alternate angle, by trying on a new lens, or uncovering the lesson from it. You learn to hold duality and you understand that all binary things in life are related.

Light amplifies the dark.

Endings are the portal to the next beginning.

Death gives birth to new life.

Sadness and joy can coexist, along with every other feeling and emotion, because they all deserve reverence. You don't have to choose!

Grief and love intertwine as one. You embrace the tears because you wholeheartedly believe that the hurt is indicative of how much you've loved.

You embrace the breaking as your invitation to venture within—to remember yourself at your essence. This is where your journey into SELF begins. Finding out who you are and what matters to you now becomes a passion—a pursuit—that guides you into the 5D.

The 5D: The Unseen World

From here, life becomes an adventure of growth and self-actualization. There is no distinction between good and bad, failure and success, or tragedy and triumph. You are the master of your own destiny because you create your reality by assigning whatever meaning you want to it.

You aren't afraid to proclaim that your loss has made you a better person and that you've been awakened by this experience. You aren't happy that your person died, but you are grateful for the experience of suffering. And you are able to own these truths about yourself because you know that your rebirth does not diminish your love for your person—it's actually connected.

In loving him

In losing him

You are who you are now.

You believe in the unseen! You allow your person's physical absence to guide you each day. You draw on the lessons you've extracted from this experience to guide each baby step—or maybe a huge leap—forward.

You believe that pain and suffering are a universal part of the human experience and that they don't minimize love, joy, and light—they amplify it. So you are no longer afraid of hardship or failure. You are your safest asset! You know that if life hands you another curveball, you will be resourceful and figure out how to adapt, and in the process, you will grow even more. You also trust that every rejection or failure—every dead end you meet—is yet another redirection to your purpose.

This invisible force is faith. It's trust in something greater, more divine, than your mind can possibly comprehend. Whether you call it God, source, creator, universe, spirit, or the knowing within YOU, there's an invisible order that connects you to the people, places, and events in your life.

Thus, we all become one. Everyone is on their individual path, yet we are at the same time connected by our pure existence. You feel more compassion and less judgment, and in doing so, you feel more inclined to celebrate your unique gifts and share them with the world. You believe that your purpose is to live your truth and seek the joy in life.

To love and love hard.

To live and live fully.

Because you know that death is the only certainty in life. So while you're in the void between this beginning and ending, you might as well live it up and THRIVE!

Grief Is Love

Dearest reader, *Love & Grief* entails lessons I learned from my own experience of loss. If something doesn't land with you right away, remember, it might just be timing.

Stay open. Stay curious. Stay connected to yourself and to others navigating the darkness (community). Allow them to hold the hope when you cannot and be your beacon of light.

I believe that thriving after a life-altering loss is possible . . . for anyone!

Admittedly, it will be easier for some of us than others, due to socioeconomic reasons, past trauma, old wounds, and conditioning (as we've discussed in depth), but having it harder is not an excuse to quit. So wherever you are in your grief journey, keep integrating. Allow this loss to change you.

If you are early on, you will resist this. You will fight like hell to keep the pre-grief version of you and all that you knew and loved in your old life. But here is my warning: *you can only swim against the current of life until you're forced under.*

Because grief is a force that is larger than you and its strength is determined by how hard you loved.

To thrive in life after loss you must allow the experience of grief, suffering, and survivorship to change you. You must enter the waters of grief and let the waves pummel you—tossing you round and round, getting scraped on the coral and cracked open like a clam shell—to eventually come out smoother and softened.

This is where I invite you reflect on everything I've shared in this book. Take a step back and become the observer of your life. Enter the realms of 4D and 5D consciousness by looking at your inner workings of the world within. Meet yourself at essence. Define what really matters. Draw on the lesson this loss has taught you, and live accordingly! With time and healing, you will discover your own truths. You will start to extract the lessons from your loss to guide you through life.

When you let your loss change you and then live in alignment with the integrated version of you, the world becomes more saturated. The blue in the sky has more meaning because you feel deep gratitude for seeing it. The green, dancing leaves have more texture and vibrance because you know that they eventually turn brown, fall to the ground and die . . . only to be reborn. The energy between family, friends, and lovers vibrates higher with hues of glittery gold and cotton-candy pink, because your heart now knows what it means to lose.

You know the tango between grief and love and you embrace the push and pull as your new love language. The pain is a part of it. Yet you're still game.

So, you choose to keep dancing!

Epilogue

❧

So there you have it! Nearly five years of lessons, tools, mindset shifts, and insights from my own personal loss. I hope that you've taken what's landed and given yourself permission to let go of the rest—because you now know that everyone's grief journey is different and . . .

You are your best guide!

I want you to know that I cried making edits to this book. I still feel grief, but it's mixed with a profound sense of gratitude. It's no longer painful; in fact, I welcome it in. It feels like a reminder of the love, the heartbreak, and everything I've walked myself through to this day.

It's still mind-boggling and bittersweet to witness bringing this book to life from the ashes of my husband's death. Prior to my loss, I never would have dreamed of becoming a published author. I had this perfect little life in a safe, contained box. When Ian died, the box was smashed into one million pieces. The walls came down, safety was lost, and my perfect little life was gone.

Yet, as I leaned into the pain, started to pick up the pieces, and rebuild my life again, I grew wiser and stronger. The walls coming down weren't just symbols of *devastation;* they were also **pathways to new possibility!** I ended up emerging from grief as someone entirely new. And as much as I loved the old box and longed to return to it at times, I knew that I could no longer fit into it. My expansion was too big to contain. And I'm hoping that after reading this book, you will believe that yours will too.

This is what happens when you survive a life-altering loss.

Death gives way to new life. **Grief is merely the portal.** So, when you find yourself stuck, looking only at the door that has closed, remember that there are likely other ones opening.

Grieve what *was*.

Accept what *is*.

Invest in what will *be*.

Not in linear stages or steps, but in the never-ending, messy, nonsensical waves and layers of grief.

And when the perfect box of your life that *was* feels too distant or out of reach, remember that you can unlock that door any time. **Simply tap into your heart!** The space where the love forever lives on. It's safe, untouchable, and forever preserved in the memories, the gratitude, and now . . . your existence moving forward.

You are your person's living legacy, and you honor them each day by choosing to LIVE in the face of death. So, wherever you are in your grief journey, remember to slow down. There is no rush to heal or move forward. Honor your own timeline and grieving style. Try not to *fight* your grief, but *flow* with it.

Remember that grief is the medicine that allows you to integrate your loss and maintain a connection to your loved one . . .

Through the love when they were living. Through the grief when they are gone.

Grief and love are one and the same.

Index

꿈

About the Author

Emily Bingham is a Certified Grief Educator, Certified Spiritual Life Coach and Grief Coach, widow, and founder of move*THRU*. After the loss of her husband in 2019 to uveal melanoma, she started her business, move*THRU*, to create new meaning out of her tragedy by helping others heal. It's now a full-blown online grief coaching business hosting a range of free content, courses, and live retreats for grievers.

Emily has worked with hundreds of clients in her private and free coaching groups and has used her story of loss to reach millions of followers through her social media content on TikTok (@emily_movesthru_grief) and Instagram (@emilypbingham). Her purpose is to help others navigating darkness seek the light by empowering them with tools, inspiration, and community.

She lives in Denver, Colorado, with her blended family of six and is thriving—soaking up the abundance, joy, and love of life!